T0129226

# Endorsements

You might have feelings of uncertainty about the future, about tomorrow, sometimes even uncertainties of the present, but Psalm 16:6 says that the Lines are fallen unto you in pleasant places and you have a Godly heritage.

In Christ you can only get better, the process may be slow, but it will only get better. My impression of Rev. Mike Rogers is, he is a man of God with a big heart, you can feel the love and optimism that flows from him. God has preserved him for such a time as this. As you read his book, every page will unfold the measure of the man.

—Rev. Dr. V.T. Williams
Bishop and Founder of Jamaica Evangelistic Association

Here is a passionate man who shares the passion of his life, Jesus.'

John F. Koeshall....God bless you and your forthcoming book, Mike. John presently in Cuiaba, Brazil.

— Dr. John F. Koeshall

For many years the Church and many Christians have maintained a Spiritual Status Quo.

However, the urgency of the times and the soon coming of the Lord has revealed that there are areas of Spiritual Maturity and development that are lacking in the Church and in individual lives today. By refusing to conform to the mold of the world, Bro Mike has opened the way for Christians to take a definite and determined stand against all the ungodly things the world says we should be or do. This book should be required reading at all ministry training centers and Bible Colleges.

— Dr. Donald Vickery Th d, SAC Cert
(Developmental Psychology)

# I Refuse to Be Who I Used to Be!

## A Conscious Decision

Stafford Michael Rogers

WESTBOW
PRESS®
A DIVISION OF THOMAS NELSON
& ZONDERVAN

Unless otherwise noted, Scripture notations are from THE NEW KING JAMES VERSION. Copyright 1979, 1980, 1982 by Thomas Nelson, Inc. Used by permission. All rights reserved.

WestBow Press books may be ordered through booksellers or by contacting:

WestBow Press
A Division of Thomas Nelson & Zondervan
1663 Liberty Drive
Bloomington, IN 47403
www.westbowpress.com
1 (866) 928-1240

ISBN: 978-1-5127-8951-5 (sc)
ISBN: 978-1-5127-8952-2 (hc)
ISBN: 978-1-5127-8950-8 (e)

Library of Congress Control Number: 2017908502

Print information available on the last page.

WestBow Press rev. date: 07/17/2017

# In the memory of Dr. Myles E. Munroe

*So many things are dropped into our lives as believers, and they often arrive in unexpected ways. Such was the case in my learning of the ministry of my dedicatee, Dr. Myles E. Munroe. Late in the year 2000 I learned of his teachings regarding the kingdom of heaven when aired on Trinity Broadcasting Network. I subsequently purchased his three-book series devoted to "Rediscovering the Kingdom" with the intention to share the treasure contained within, in an adult Sunday School setting. I penned a letter to TBN thanking them for airing the ten-episode teaching and followed with a copy of that letter to Dr. Munroe. I received a personal reply (not a form letter) From Dr. Munroe.* Get this! This is a man who has been in the presence of, and advisor to kings, prime ministers, and other leaders of nations of the world, and he continued to personally answer his mail! I was further very deeply impacted by his comment that he felt confident that the richest place on our planet is the cemetery, that in it are the dreams of businesses that were never started, inventions that were never copyrighted, songs that were never penned, and books left unwritten. At that moment I felt the confirming tug that I was to follow the earlier prompting of the Holy Spirit and begin to compile the words for this manuscript. I learned of the passing of Dr. Munroe and his beloved wife Ruth on November 9, 2014 and am certain that his all encompassing dissemination of Jesus's central and pivotal message, "The Gospel of the Kingdom" through the many Spirit-driven seminars, manuscripts and visual media will continue to produce fruit until the return of Jesus, the Great King. Dr. Munroe never rose too high to forget the days of small things (Zechariah 4:10). Admirable, and so reminiscent of the truly incomparable king that I have chosen to revere.

Thank you, Dr. Munroe.

# Prologue

I have recently been strongly led to know more of the wonderful and often indescribable activities that are available to every sincere seeker of Christ who is totally dedicated and determined to press in until a previously unknown and frankly unimagined level of spiritual intimacy is achieved. I have been taught, then understood, and now have experienced for several years that the Holy Spirit is constantly revealing and speaking of the thoughts, desires, and direction that the heavenly Father wishes to fully extend into the earthly realm ("Thy kingdom come"). I have, however, been "as a child" in my efforts to attain an ever-present intimacy (*yada*, Hebrew) and walk (a lifestyle) with the Lord through the teaching, directing, and guidance of the person of the Holy Spirit. I recognize that He has been consistently present, but I unfortunately have been distracted, preoccupied, or, worse, insensitive to His gentle yet coaxing and persistent presence.

Oh, on a few occasions, He has been able to penetrate my crusty exterior and impress me that I need to go to the mirror and see the person responsible for most of the difficulties in my life (the responses I give to what life tosses at me). Additionally I am to have compassion on the multitude by looking deep into their eyes, seeing the pain, and listening to the words that come from their lips to receive clues as to how I can be a servant-minister to their deepest need. I am ashamed to now realize and confess the perhaps immeasurable quantity of opportunity that I have missed due primarily to my failure to refuse to be satisfied with the status quo and instead to stir up myself to deepen my intimate fellowship with the Lord Jesus Christ through the person of the Holy Spirit.

The good news of course is that He is patient, merciful, and tenacious, and as a result, He has seen fit to place directly into my path (Ps. 16:11; Prov. 3:5–6) many teachers/ministers with vision for God's dream and my destiny to be fully accomplished. These include Dr. Heidi Baker, Christine Caine, Graham Cooke, Paul Keith Davis, Dr. Dick Eastman, James Goll, Dr. John Hash, Dr. Jack Hayford, John Paul Jackson, Cindy Jacobs, Bill Johnson, Rick Joiner, Bob Jones, Patricia King, Dr. Caroline Leaf, Zola Levitt, Campbell McAlpine, Dr. G. Campbell Morgan, Dr. Myles E. Munroe, Chuck Pierce, Larry Randolph, Dutch Sheets, Steve Thompson, Lance Wallnau, John Wimber, and Ravi Zacharias.

This group and obviously many others have propelled the twenty-first-century church into the understanding needed to recognize that Jesus came to earth to restore the kingdom that satan had stolen in the garden. Jesus announced this in Matthew 4:17 when he began His ministry, and He later notified His followers that the time of the end and His subsequent return would not occur until His message ("the gospel of the kingdom") had been preached unto all nations as a witness (Matt. 24:14).

For my part, it seems that the most efficient and effective way to accomplish the task at hand is to dive headlong into previously uncharted depths of intimate relationship of which I am sure that few, if any of us, yet realize the full implication. Of this one thing I am certain, my purest intentions are to be among:

- those whose soul "follows hard after thee" (Ps. 63:8);
- those who are determined to "be still and know" that He is God (Ps. 46:10); and
- those who, like Moses (Ex. 3:3–4), will turn aside from the routine, mundane activities and see what God is doing at any given moment and,
- those who like the apostle Paul, fervently desire "that I may know Him" (Phil. 3:10).

In short, I refuse to be who I used to be! How about you? Do you care to come aboard for the journey of your life? By the way, it is only fair that I caution you that this journey is one day at a time, one step at a time, for a lifetime, or until Christ's second return. To each of you who are willing to overtly make such a conscious decision, I joyfully proclaim and welcome aboard! Please rest assured that you will never regret this extravagant determination.

# Acknowledgments

When I recall that I am a composite of all the people I have met, known, and learned from, it appears that it has taken more than seventy years to prepare me for—and more than eight of those years to prompt me to—write this offering. There were times when much of the content lay untouched for months. There were, however, also more than a few occurrences when friends, associates, coworkers, and fellow believers made thoughtful, complimentary comments concerning their perception of a heavenly gifting they felt I had been given that enabled me to write, which they had based upon a letter of encouragement or recommendation, a greeting card, or congratulatory document I had written.

Their comments were genuinely appreciated and certainly instrumental in leading me to continue to press on; however, four even more intimate motivators must not go unrecognized.

The first was/is a constant source of encouragement and, if you can receive it, even more intimate. With the greatest respect and affection, I call Him "the hound of heaven." He, the Holy Spirit, is ever with me, and He keeps me constantly in contact with Jesus who is one with the Father. Simply knowing that the entirety of the resources of heaven are ever accessible is consistent stimulus to achieve all that is needed.

The second is my wife Cindy assuredly an Heaven sent treasure that consistently intercedes, encourages, suggests, counsels, celebrates, and perceptively shares Holy Spirit driven understanding of Kingdom concepts with such depth of insight that I frequently find myself thinking, oh, how I wish I had said that.

The third is my mother, most certainly a woman of prayer and assuredly a student of God's Word. I owe her a debt of gratitude that I cannot repay by any quantity of the most extravagant heartfelt words that I might be capable of uttering. Nevertheless, I am certain that the Lord has exceeded her every expectation by the fulfillment of the promise of Psalm 17:15, her very favorite verse, "As for me, I will see your face in righteousness; I shall be satisfied when I awake in your likeness." And as I once youthfully scrawled in one of my earliest Bibles,

"I Love My Mom."

Mike held by Mom, grandma Fannie looking on.

The fourth and by no means the least, is my earthly father whose work ethic was so very commendable and instrumental in forming mine. I recall so many instances where he was quite congested and so fevered that he had every right to have stayed in bed, or as a minimum to have gotten an injection, but his consistent response was predictably the same,"Oh, horse feathers, I'll just sweat it out", and off he would go to work high above the ground in the tower of an oil-drilling rig which frequently included driving more than 50 miles each way.

Thank you Dad, for this laudable lifestyle. Those are some huge shoes to fill.

Mike wearing his father's shoes

# Introduction

The reason that you have continued to read this far is that you have not yet secured the deepest longing inside you. You have searched unsuccessfully for inexpressible joy, for limitless fulfillment while exploring every path that might lead to your greatest expectation. Yet this dream continues to be just beyond your farthest reach. You have memory of that dream, perhaps it was a series of childhood interactions with your beloved grandmother, her smile that dwells in the recesses of your heart, her whispers that brought forth multiple giggles, the loving incomparable touch that continues to tug at your heartstrings and those unforgettable freshly baked cookies whose fragrance will not fade from your memory... or perhaps it was the series of one-on-one moments with your father where he took you step-by-step through the necessary sequences of preparing for the impending hunt; the disassembly, lubrication, reassembling and subsequent target practice while gently describing the necessity of a good sight picture and the squeezing of the trigger...such intimate times of celebration are irreplaceable as are those spent with your very best friend, you know those moments... it's just the two of you, you share your innermost secrets, and uncontainable joy floods throughout your every cell, the continuous laughter, the affectionate touches, the glowing smiles, while in indescribable expectation you can hardly wait until your next intimate session with this gift that most closely represents your deepest need for human friendship. The one shortcoming of this invaluable relationship is that this superb friend cannot be with you every moment of each day. But, the extravagantly good news is that the actual best friend who created us is available at all times and under every circumstance to show us the daily path that will direct us to a life of super abundance, and in whose presence is fullness of joy, and at whose right hand can be found, pleasures evermore. The subject of your search is described in the very last verse of Psalm sixteen and throughout the pages of this offering. Eureka.

# Chapter 1—Transitioning Preparatory School

My favorite moment is when I look into the eyes of the person in front of me and see a warm glow in the same eyes that a few moments before were lifeless pools of emptiness. From their lips flow words of hope that replaced those recently spoken that seemed to have been driven by such disappointing, even cruel despair.

Please know that these priceless moments weren't always my quest. It had mostly been all about me. Compassion for the multitude was to arrive many years later and only after a very extensive change. So just how did this come to be?

The prep school began in July 1941 when a twenty-two-year-old mother took her ten-day-old son to the front of the small neighborhood mission in downtown San Antonio for the express purpose of presenting him to the Lord to be used as one of His servants for as many years as were granted to him. The young mother was a relative newcomer to Christian service, having been led to a life of faith in the Lord Jesus Christ by her sister-in-law just slightly more than one year before.

Her mother had passed away four years earlier after being bedridden for several years. As a result of the extended infirmity, the family had no history of church attendance, let alone any exposure to a relationship with the Lord. Her father had worked long hours farming the family plot near

Benton City, Texas, a sparsely settled farming community a few miles southeast of Lytle. Her grandmother, a spirit-filled, tongue-talking Methodist, was known to walk the streets of Lytle witnessing to all who would listen, which included frequently and openly worshiping in her heavenly language. She died, however, before she could leave her spiritual mark on her granddaughter.

My confidence in God's faithfulness to honor the grandmother's heavenly relationship convinces me that He placed a deposit in the heart of this young mother so, when her sister-in-law began to share with her the incalculable value of Jesus's gift, she recognized the witness to be truth and thus joyfully received it.

The days passed, and the young mother, nicknamed Jo, faithfully attended the services at her local church and had such a hunger for more of God that she frequently traveled around South Texas to revival meetings. Her child Mike was always with her, sitting beside her with her arm around his shoulders, gently caressing him, and applying correction as needed, while he was consistently exposed to the presence of the Holy Spirit.

Jo had said on more than a few occasions that she wanted to shape Mike into the perfect child, but all who had known him could attest to the fact that result didn't occur, as Jo was to later learn.

Approximately two months after his fourth birthday, Mike ran a fever of 106 degrees. It lasted for more than thirty hours despite his mother's efforts to lower it using ice packs, cold water towels, and alcohol baths. In those days, medical doctors still made house calls, so Jo asked her four-year-old son if he wanted her to call the doctor or follow scripture and call for the local church elders to come anoint him with oil and pray for the manifestation of his healing. Mike opted for the elders.

They arrived soon after the call, and fewer than two minutes after the anointing/prayer, his body temperature returned to normal, and the youngster was soon enthusiastically swinging on his new rocking horse swing that his grandfather had gotten him for his fourth birthday.

The point worth noting is that the lifestyle demonstrated by a spiritually inexperienced mother had dramatically impacted the life of her firstborn in just four short years.

So where was Mike's dad in all of this? He was raised at Ditto, also a small farming community, near Poteet, Texas in similar spiritual environs as the boy's mom. His family had been so busy with daily farming that they also had failed to demonstrate any consistent proclivity for church attendance, let alone any close relationship with the Lord. They did profess to be Baptist in their belief structure but provided little evidence of consistent devotion, not unlike many families in America today.

Stat, as Dad was known, was now actively into breadwinning first via selling hardware, next as a bread salesman, and later as a bus operator for the city of San Antonio until the lure of the oil patch manifested itself. The attraction of this higher income source lured Stat and started him on an adventure that would lead his family to several cities in South Texas—Lytle, George West, Three Rivers, Eagle Pass, Cotulla, and Pettus—in short, wherever the oil "bidness" (sic) was happening. The benefits of this frequent relocation was a harvest of so very many acquaintances, several good friends, and the techniques needed to make friends.

My first unforgettable friend was named Gene Howard. The years were 1947 to 1952, and the place was Lytle. I can't fully define why there's such special affinity for some people, but it does occur (for example, the psalmist/later king David and Jonathan, son of King Saul). It wasn't the nine-inch Dumont black-and-white, round-tubed television at his home, although I certainly enjoyed watching *Howdy Doody*, *Sky King*, *Buffalo Bob*, and all the cowboy westerns on the one channel. (That's correct, folks, there was only one TV channel.) Frankly, I can't recall the name of even one toy or game he had, but I do clearly cherish the memories of those days as though it were yesterday.

I would go over to his house after school or on Saturdays, and then as the shadows of the day lengthened, Mother would call, reminding me to come home for dinner. Every time I would plead, "Mom, can't I please stay just a little longer with my friend?" (Many years later this was to become my heart cry for extended time with my most intimate friend, Jesus of Nazareth, lately of heaven).

A few years later while in Cotulla, I was the beneficiary of yet another unforgettable friend, John Lewis. Our birthdays were exactly three months apart (to the day), but in many ways, we were different. He was quiet; I was a loudmouth.

4

He was studious; I was a laid back student. He was cultured; I was country. But our differences proved advantageous for both of us.

John introduced me to classical music such as Bach, Beethoven, Brahms, Ravel, Respighi, Rossini, and Tschaikovsky et al. He loved the famed and fiery conductor Arturo Toscanini and would stand for hours on end in front of his RCA Hi-Fi Consolette with baton in hand passionately directing symphony after symphony.

He and his mother took me to my first symphonic outing performed by the San Antonio symphony with Harvey Biskin, tympanist (a John favorite). And then we went to the first class St. Anthony Hotel and and an introduction to my first baked Alaska dessert. Oh,my! Luscious.

John loved Winston Churchill, and I can still hear the LP (33 1/3 RPM, long-play) recordings of Churchill's exhortations ringing in my inner ear of memory. I just knew John would be published one day. He was on the high school annual staff. Military school and college were already fully determined on his horizon, and oh, how he relished history.

I remember the celebration when his mother was first published in the *New Yorker* magazine, and through her connections, they procured an autograph from J. Frank Dobie for my copy of *The Longhorns*. I recall as though it were yesterday when John and I crawled out his second-story bedroom window, sat on the roof, and watched the Russian Sputnik catapult the world into the space age. John would later write extensively about the "Cold War" era.

John wanted to improve his English scores, and I didn't like biology, so we coached and quizzed each other to much improved scores. When we learned that my family would be moving to Pettus at midterm of my junior year, John set up a surprise going-away party (think shock & awe), one I won't forget. As the yearbook editor, he had several of the photos placed in it. And that party was truly an unforgettable surprise!

You might be wondering why in the world I would include these two vignettes about Gene and John. Well, here's the reason, and don't forget it. I don't have the same clothes, houses, guns, bling, or cars I once owned. They've all gone by the wayside. But you never forget your best friends. Relationships are the most important things. Life isn't about collecting stuff. It's actually about establishing and nurturing friendships.

Please know as well that you can prevent or reduce the possibility, in fact the likelihood, of loneliness during your senior years by creating treasured moments during your first fifty years. And should you already be past the fifty-year mark, it's not too late to begin.

Call someone you know and respect, perhaps from afar, and invite this person out for dinner, your treat. Get this individual to talk about himself or herself, and simply listen to him or her. Smile at appropriate times, ask clarifying questions to communicate genuine interest, and be determined to initiate a relaxed and unhurried event. And don't forget the cocoanut cream pie or the the peach cobbler, or perhaps both?

At the end, look this person straight in the eye, and genuinely and generously thank him or her for an unforgettable evening. You won't regret the investment, and this may become the first of many more to follow. The importance of such an occasion cannot be overemphasized.

Also during these follow-the-oil-patch years we—my mother, my sister Beverly, and me—were able to travel and attend many wonderful gatherings of fellow worshippers with an exposure to a plethora of spiritual activity. This included attendance of tent revival meetings of the likes of A. A. Allen, Jack Coe, Gayle Jackson, and Oral Roberts. Funny how you don't see the true value of all that until years later, as you view it through life's rearview mirror. I really missed that all of this was a grand design by the awesome creator of the universe. He enabled me to easily meet folks and eventually to unapologetically share His extravagant news with them.

We actually had a three-year pause in George West/Three Rivers from 1952 to 1955 where a Pentecostal guitar-picking minister named Hansel Gene Byars took me under his wing and demonstrated many basic and several advanced techniques of rhythm and chording, yet another skill attained for future use. He was "instrumental" in helping my parents choose my 1940's era arched-top Gibson guitar. I shall not forget this unselfish most-extravagant gift.

In the summer of 1955, the oil patch took the family to Eagle Pass, and we chose to attend a church in a nearby hamlet named Quemado, Spanish for "burnt." During that time, our multitasking Sunday school teacher and youth/children leader, Sister Jewell Stock, challenged each of us to memorize the names of the sixty-six books of the Bible with the promise of a rainbow Bible if we were successful. I had no clue that, starting some twenty-five years later, I would be using this newfound knowledge for the balance of my life. Once again, I was being prepared (or set up) by the Lord for his future use. Much later I was to learn that the Lord was preparing me for something that He already had prepared for me, His spiritual blueprint of my life, if you will, my destiny.

A year later, the summer of 1956 actually, we moved to Cotulla, and while attending church in nearby Dilley, the opportunity came to attend a youth church camp at Singing Hills Camp (a Ranch) near the hamlet of Concan. The event was enjoyable, and my autograph book was signed by fellow attendees, some of which would not be seen again until more than forty years later at Hillcrest Church in Seguin (I still have that autograph book, relationships are absolutely essential).

I'd like to say that a call to ministry was placed on my life at that camp, but such was not the case. There was, however, an additional occurrence while living in Cotulla that had great significance and potentially life-altering consequences. Mother had learned of a revival event to be held near Corpus Christi and felt a strong pull to attend. She came to me and suggested we might attend. I was sixteen years of age. I so enjoyed (still do) to witness gifted musicians, vocalists, and their anointed joy-filled offerings. And need I mention that there was a strong likelihood that there would be more than a few "nice to look at" young ladies there.

But even with all of this positive attraction, I had a check in my spirit. I didn't know why, and my mom, who knew me very well, was quite surprised. Frankly I was the most surprised as the words, "I don't know why, but I just don't feel like I should go this time," came off my lips.

Well, Mother and Beverly set out for Corpus Christi, and less than one hour after they departed, near the small town of Tilden, a deer crossed the path of the vehicle, and in the process of braking and avoidance, the deer struck the front of the automobile, causing it to turn over at least three times before coming to a rest. There were only lap (seat) belts in those days, and due to the size of my six-foot-three-inch frame, I very probably would have been in the backseat to assure better leg room. And who knows what might have resulted? The good news is that Mother and Beverly were protected and experienced only the soreness that occurs with such trauma.

Let me assure you that today I know the one who knows, and three of my life verses say it far better than I ever could:

- "You will show me the PATH of life" (Ps. 16:11; Acts 2:28).
- "Trust in the Lord with ALL your heart … and He shall direct your PATHS" (Prov. 3:5–6).
- "And the STEPS of a good man are ordered of the Lord" (Ps. 37:23).

Need I say more?

As you may already have guessed, it's time to move once again, this time to Pettus at midterm 1958. Coincidently (and likely another God setup), an English/drama professor from Texas Tech University who was seeking a break from the demands of the hectic college pace decided to accept a one-year hiatus by applying for and accepting an offer to teach English grammar. Since I had just completed grammar at Cotulla, this college professor designed an English literature curriculum just for my edification.

Being a drama major himself, Bill Martin began to stretch the mind of this small town eleventh grader by leading him into an appreciation and understanding of William Shakespeare, poetry, and college-level classics. In a few short weeks, this teacher got this boy to agree to participate in a UIL (University Interscholastic League) poetry reciting competition.

And the point of this? I would later learn that this speaking in a public forum before both educators and my peers was again to prepare me for a future role as a teacher of the word. But more about that later.

You might ask, "Why then was this even mentioned? Was it just to satisfy some latent ego activity?"

No, actually it is included with the hope that you might retrospectively see some similar and perhaps seemingly unimportant events in your own experience that were actually a part of the grand design to prepare you to achieve the destiny that had been planned for you even before your birth was contemplated.

May I be so bold as to remind you that it should be no surprise to any of us that there are no coincidences in the life of any true follower of Christ. All we need know is that God has full knowledge of the preappointed times and the boundaries of the dwellings of every person of every nation on the earth (Acts 17:26). It's not that we are puppets forced into a predetermined path. Rather, as free moral agents, we have chosen to accept His path that He has custom-designed for each of us. Our decision to trust in the Lord with all our heart and to lean not to our own understanding and in all our ways to acknowledge Him and He shall direct our paths (Prov. 3:5-6) makes it so wonderfully obvious that our times and boundaries are known in advance by Him that knows the end from the beginning.

While Mr. Martin never directly referred to salvation, he posed such poignant questions as, "Mike, as far as we can see, there are suns, moons, stars, and galaxies. What's beyond all that?" That profound question destroyed my existing lines of mental limitations regarding the unimaginable vastness of God's six days of original creation. I experienced an immediate explosion of broad spectrum growth.

And if that were not enough, he further encouraged me to read John Bunyan's *Pilgrim's Progress* and introduced me to the works of William Cowper and G. K. Chesterton. In short, he clearly pointed me into a considered direction.

Permit me to declare that Bill Martin had, by far, the most profound impact of any educator during the first eighteen years of my life. True, he was extremely bright, but of far greater importance, he cared! He cared enough to write in my yearbook that he saw me as an outstanding student, specifically the Latin phrase *sui generis* (in a class by himself) as his assessment.

This is so impacting that, fifty-eight years later, it still has unforgettable import. To every teacher, which obviously begins with our parents, I say, "Be encouraged and know that what you do and say has profound and lifelong significance." This may seem to be quite obvious, but you are truly a most significant component in their experiential path. Rest assured that every negative word you utter has the potential of everlasting debilitating effects. Please...please, PLEASE use great care before speaking any words while in a state of frustration or anger.

So high school graduation came on May 22, 1959, and I completed one semester of college at Del Mar in Corpus Christi until the lure of my own career/cash/benefits/ retirement pulled me to work at Sears, Roebuck & Company, and that was until I received Uncle Sam's "Greetings, your neighbors have selected you" notice in November 1963.

And since I preferred to choose my military training specialty, I decided to visit my local recruiter and ask him to bargain with my draft board with the understanding that I would enlist for four years rather than serve the customary two-year draft stint.

He asked if I had opened my letter notifying me of my draft call, and when I answered in the affirmative, he forewarned me that there was actually no chance that they would agree to this. But they did! (In retrospect, this undoubtedly was a heaven driven result!).

Please bear with me a bit as I develop this, as I fully expect that you might be surprised at the series of events that occurred as a result. I was assigned to basic training at Fort Leonard Wood, Missouri (AKA Fort lost-in-the woods, in the state of misery, chuckle) where I was selected to be the guidon bearer (the soldier who carries the flag up front) for Company C, 1st Battalion, 2nd Training Regiment, Basic.

After basic training, I received my advanced training in communications at Fort Devens in Ayer, Massachusetts, and subsequently was assigned to serve overseas at Kagnew Station in Asmara, Eritrea, Ethiopia, East Africa.

The body of water adjacent to the coast at Massawa, Ethiopia, is the Red Sea. The sovereign of Ethiopia at that time was His Imperial Majesty Haile Selassie, believed by many Ethiopians to be a direct-line descendant of King Solomon and the Queen of Sheba. Some Ethiopians and some Bible scholars maintain that, where God's Word declares that Solomon gave the queen "the desires of her heart," a child birthed of that acquaintance was King Menelik, from whom His Imperial Majesty Haile Selassie directly descended.

A town in northern Ethiopia, Axum (Aksum), contains a church named St. Mary's of Zion. An in-residence lifetime service priest watches over the facility and its contents. Upon request, the crowns of the previous monarchs of Ethiopia were brought out of the church and displayed for viewing, but not touching. It is also claimed by many Ethiopians and believed by some scholars that the original ark of the covenant resides in the basement of this church. It has been stated by some that, when King Solomon became more interested in collecting chariots, horses, wives, concubines, and wealth than in his relationship with Jehovah, a duplicate ark of the covenant was crafted. The Queen of Sheba purchased it— and some think Solomon may have given it to her, per "the desires of her heart"—and transported the original back to Ethiopia.

No, we were not shown the ark; nor was any mention of this made at the time of our visit to Axum. I have only heard of this in recent years. So during my twice-extended tour, a total of thirty-seven months, in Ethiopia, His Imperial Majesty visited us, and our post commander directed that a full honor guard be displayed for Haile Selassie. Care to guess who was the company guidon bearer for the honor guard? Coincidence? Not in my mind. Additionally we were granted a private audience with the king and his entourage and permitted to ask questions. Yes, he spoke English. In fact English, at his directive, was a required subject in their schools.

What I now want to confess is that I was not honoring the Lord during these thirty-seven months. Quite the contrary. My participation in three secular bands was cheapening my guitar and vocal talents, yet God was preparing me (another setup?) for a future time when I would come to myself and make a conscious decision to pursue the destiny that He had in mind for me before my earthly existence.

Of course the real question continued to be how much longer I would tramp around in the wilderness before I recognized and rejected the deception of the enemy. As you hopefully are very well aware:

> *The destructive dilemma of deception is that, when you're deceived, you don't recognize that you have been deceived, because you ARE deceived.* Selah, 1 Cor. 2:14

Does any of this sort of rearview mirror activity seem even vaguely familiar to your early years? No doubt, your circumstances might have been different, and your activities could well have varied from those just described. But with careful consideration, can you now perceive some very obvious events in your past that were no less important in establishing the direction you were to go while all the time preparing and providing you with the understanding, experience, knowledge, wisdom, skills, and resources that would enable you to make a both conscious and crucial determination to achieve the destiny set before you, a future planned, yes, even before your birth was contemplated?

Please allow me to strongly encourage you, if you are not already in the pursuit of the fulfillment of your destiny, that you begin to formulate a plan today and to follow Habakkuk's exhortation (2:2) to "write the vision; and make it plain on tablets that he (THAT "he" also includes you- author) may run who reads it" and declaring aloud that you will begin today, not one of these days, to passionately launch out into previously uncharted spiritual waters by

- totally immersing yourself in His Word (2 Tim 2:15);
- being still until you "know" (Ps. 46:10) that He is God;
- continuously "hosting" His presence (Ex. 33:14–15; Ps. 16:11);
- allowing Him to show you great and hidden things through ongoing daily conversation (prayer) (Jer. 33:3); and
- consistently telling Him that, while you are most appreciative of everything He has already done, you are not satisfied.

You want more. In fact, you want all He has prepared for you, and in so doing, you can avoid the many examples of poor personal choices that have been documented throughout this volume. My sincere prayer is that the contents of this offering will serve to be an extraordinarily powerful stimulus that results in your intentional, conscious decision to reject the status quo that is so prevalent today and determine to stir up yourself to achieve the fulfillment of your God-planned destiny and realize that this understanding will ultimately enable you to declare, with reasonable confidence, the words of Jesus as recorded in John 17:4, "I have glorified you on the earth, I have finished the work which you have given me to do."

You are already well aware that there is clearly no satisfaction in settling for the so-called status quo. It leaves you so totally unfulfilled, agreed? So why not step forward armed with the declaration spoken by Jesus in Matthew 11:11b and repeated in Luke 7:28b where He states, "Assuredly, I say to you, among those born of women there has not risen one greater than John the Baptist; but who is least in the kingdom of heaven is greater than he." John was the last of the old covenant prophets and was honored to herald the advent of the new covenant which brought the advantages of Christ's gifts provided through His crucifixion, death, burial, resurrection, and the advent of the Holy Spirit which ushered in the reality of the new covenant kingdom. This "greater than he" declaration accentuates the increased value of the new covenant above that of the first (old) covenant. Thus those who have received Christ and the accompanying advantages are members of the new covenant kingdom and are therefore equipped to do the works that Jesus did which are greater than those of the first covenant (John 14:12) and is why those who are the least in the kingdom of heaven are greater than John the Baptist. What a difference the fulfillment of Acts 1:8 (*dunamis* power, Greek) makes, not only in our afterlife but in our day-to-day living out the lifestyle of an ambassador (2 Cor. 5:20), one that carries the portfolio of the Great King and chooses to be a bond servant of our fellow man in this current and temporary realm in which we find ourselves. (Please note that Ambassadors do not express personal opinions, they only declare the positions stated by their government. So, as representatives of the kingdom of heaven, we simply must solely share the portfolio of heaven, God's declared Word.)

Such a powerful determination will be enabled by the King of Glory from whom comes every good gift and every perfect gift (James 1:17). The ability to accomplish this new choice will be delivered via the indwelling and empowering person named the Holy Spirit. And because the Holy Spirit only communicates what He hears from Jesus and recalling that Jesus only did and said what He saw the Father doing/ saying, you can be certain that you will be doing the exact will of the Father. And doesn't that certainty bring fullness of joy and incomparable pleasure evermore?

# Chapter 2—Separation, a Road to Damascus

It's now October 1967, and I am honorably discharged from the United States Army and decide to return to San Antonio to reclaim my job at Sears, Roebuck & Company and proceed to seek my fame and fortune in the wonderful world of retail. I take the many necessary steps to get promoted from department to department by availing myself of all the pertinent corporate correspondence courses that the then "World's Largest Retailer" had to offer.

I was chosen to fill several of those not so glamorous assignments as well as some of the more desirable jobs. Additionally I was selected to chauffeur the wife of the big boss to the dentist, medical doctor, luxury retail stores, and so forth. In short, I was doing whatever was necessary to climb the corporate ladder as rapidly as possible. So for twenty-two years, I did all the stuff and ascended the ladder from selling Craftsman tools for $1.25 an hour to ultimately becoming a store manager over commercial sales and leading a store staff of twenty-eight persons.

It all came crashing down in May 1982 when I was discharged (fired) for approving an unauthorized credit sale, an exact action that my previous "big boss" had done and for which he was not discharged.

But now the sales tide had slowed, we were top-heavy with tenured executives, and Walmart (the next "World's

Largest Retailer") loomed large on the retail horizon. I was quite expensive. I was soon to receive five weeks of vacation and a five-to-one company distribution in my profit-sharing account. So I walked out the front door of the building with a cardboard box filled with national trophies, awards, and plaques. And then I realized I had been climbing the wrong ladder. I had been following the wrong "star." But don't think for a moment that a loving, caring, and awesome God had forsaken me. No, no, no. Quite the contrary.

You see, exactly one month (to the day) earlier, I was motoring to Corpus Christi to implement some updated training when, with absolutely no effort and no seeking on my part, I was very powerfully overcome by the presence of the Lord. Tears that felt like hot molten lead and which seemed to be the size of silver dollars began to flow profusely. I was not living a life pleasing to the Lord and certainly was undeserving of such a cleansing action.

I have subsequently learned through query that the prayers of my godly mother and her prayer partners had been storming heaven on my behalf. A mercy-filled and caring God of grace had responded as only He can. I can assure you with absolute certainty that I was no longer the same, rather "turned into another man" (1 Sam. 10:6) when I arrived in Corpus Christi, which, by the way, means "body of Christ." Hmm, just consider that. An eternal deposit of desire for total transformation had been credited to my account, no doubt about it.

I chose to select as the title for this chapter the definition of "separation/division" because I feel so certain that the Lord was redirecting my path from the broad way to a straight and narrow path (Matt. 7:13–14). Our Abba Father is so fully committed to His promise of being unwilling that "any should perish but that all should come to repentance" (2 Peter 3:9), which includes every wayward prodigal, He will, as He did to Saul of Tarsus, knock us off our "lofty perch" (Acts 9:4) to redirect us to that straight and narrow path of life.

I certainly didn't deserve it, but for some reason, He somehow seems to think I am worth it, "Behold what manner of love" (1 John 3:1). His love is far beyond my ability to fully measure. I am totally convinced that we just do not fully perceive the magnitude of it. And if you have been looking for a genuine love, only to be disappointed time after time, please be assured that, if you will sincerely turn to this greatest lover of all time (John 3:16; 1 John 4:8, 16) and give Him full charge of your life, He will enable you to locate the human who will reciprocate with the respect and love you have so deeply craved and so unsuccessfully sought.

Hint: it is highly unlikely that this person will be discovered in a bar, nightclub, or dance hall, as almost every one of those potential candidates are also looking for love in all the wrong places and are as well, carrying many of the same frustrations, disappointments, failures, and lack of fulfillment that you have endured, because we frequently approximate those with whom we associate. Or in the vernacular of South Texas, we most often become like those with whom we "hang out." Additionally God's everlasting and undying love will sustain you in the daily times of tribulation, a "two-dollar" word for the ongoing trouble that accompanies our daily living (John 16:33). Simply stated, it's time for each of us to stop looking for love in all the wrong places.

So what's to be done when the God of creation shows up and so clearly demonstrates such incomparable love? For me, it was time to make a conscious decision to pursue Him. I headed to a Dick Eastman Change the World School of Prayer (World Literature Crusade) conference at Trinity Church in San Antonio.

In that seminar, Dick (Now Dr.) introduced us to an excellent Bible devotional/study guide called "The Bible

Pathway," which we learned would guide us through the entire Bible annually by reading approximately fifteen minutes a day. Let me just tell you that I'm the kind of guy that, if I say I might try something, I will never get it done. If, however, I say I'm going to do it, that is to say, a conscious decision, it will happen (Think, hard-headed Scotch-Irish boy).

I have now read through the Bible more than twenty-eight times, and this journey has led me to additionally pursue the spiritual understanding of so many determined seekers of the atmosphere of heaven acquired by them through their ongoing intimate heavenly relationships with Abba Father, His Beloved Son, and the brilliant communicator-enabler Holy Spirit, which includes but is not limited to teachers such as John Wimber, Lester Sumrall, Dr. Jack Hayford, J. Vernon McGee, Dr. G. Campbell Morgan, Dr. Myles E. Munroe, Mario Murillo, Derek Prince, Dr. Ed Young, Ravi Zacharias, Jack Graham, Dutch Sheets, Dr. Caroline Leaf, Bill Johnson, Graham Cooke, and, of course, the most brilliant of all time, one Jesus of Nazareth, lately of heaven.

This trek has catapulted me into an ongoing pursuit of the knowledge, understanding, and wisdom of the Christ, which has presently led into an insatiable hunger for relationship. I cannot overstate the importance nor insist too strongly the value and quantity of encouragement of having a devotional that daily guides you into the Word and prayer and ultimately into His indescribable presence. Please know that a devotional is used as a supplement to assist in acquiring basic understanding and for clarifying difficult passages thereby drawing us further into the concealed matters of God (Prov. 25:2) and is never meant to become a substitute for daily immersion in His Word.

But how did I arrive here? It hasn't happened overnight and certainly not without much failure and many poor choices on my part that brought about considerable pain, suffering, and further disappointment, to wit, a failed marriage of twenty-seven-plus years caused by my poor choices including, but not limited to, the choice to be unequally yoked together; the resulting pain, suffering, and disappointment associated with many other foolish (sin-borne) choices initiated by me during that marriage; and, if that were not enough, an additional, subsequent failed relationship. Would I ever learn?

Does any of this sound painfully familiar? I wasn't content to let it stop there. Oh no! I made successive sinful choices that led to further pain, which included indebtedness. But you know what? Here came the faithful God of eternity once again to pick me up, forgive me, and restore me (Gal. 6:1) and relocate me to a place where He could get my undivided attention.

Oh, I thought I was going to Seguin,Texas, to be near my aging parents, but He had His own plans (Think, "Jehovah Sneaky)! So I ended up in a ten-by-fifty house trailer in a mobile home park, alone with God, my Bible, and Christian television, specifically Dr. Myles Munroe, Mario Murillo, PTL television network, and others. In short, I was in a God-controlled environment where He had my full attention. Simply stated I would go to work daily and then return home to be led into intimate relationship with the true and living God.

If you have been in one of these trailers, you know that on one side of the tiny kitchen sink there is frequently about three or so inches of space. I had placed a napkin in that space with a handwritten earnest request for Him to cleanse me, change me, reshape me, mold me, and put me on His potter's wheel, in short, the Romans 12:1–2 metamorphosis.

Let me just assure you that, when you make such a request, you have chosen to fully surrender to His leading and He honors the request. And because He is just, He will do ALL that is required to enable you to achieve it. And while it is typically so very uncomfortable, this metamorphosis (renaissance) is absolutely necessary and ultimately so very rewarding. As I invited Him to recycle me and after months of restoration and very many sessions of intimacy with Him, I was led to accept a Sunday school substitute- teacher assignment.

In 1998, I also began to assist the youth pastor, Bobby Nixon (presently my senior pastor at Hope Church in La Vernia, Texas) in the vagaries of that youthful, exciting, and rewarding ministry and subsequently became known as the self-proclaimed "world's oldest teenager." As Proverbs 23:7 says, "For as he thinks in his heart so is he." And yes, that guitar ability was again called into ongoing use; however, this time it would be to honor the giver of every good gift (James 1:17).

As a result of serving in the youth ministry, in 2000 I was invited to be the Bible guy at a weekly Bible study in the detached garage of a private residence. The typical attendance was about seven, including me, of which two were the teenage daughters of the single-parent owner of the residence.

During this time, my niece Candace informed me of the scheduled visit of Reverend Derek Prince at Cornerstone Church in San Antonio. Being somewhat familiar with his ministry from the 1970s, I decided to attend the service and subsequently asked the two teenage daughters if they felt that their mother might be interested in attending as well. They indicated they thought she might be and surprisingly commented that the three of them had previously discussed the possibility of attending, but their mother didn't relish the idea of the extended trip to San Antonio and even less the late evening return drive back to Seguin.

So having briefly met their mother at church and actually regularly attending the adult Bible class of which she was a faithful participant, I asked if she and her daughters would consider accompanying me to the service. She indicated they would. I was single, as was she, but I truly wasn't trying to use this as an excuse to meet her. I will readily admit, however, that once you have been involved in youth ministry for a considerable time, you do appreciate some adult conversation along the way. (No offense intended, my fellow teenagers.)

The service was absolutely delightful, the presence of the Holy Spirit moved so powerfully, and many attendees were quite inarguably delivered from the throes of the enemy. After the service, we stopped at a nearby restaurant and had fellowship while enjoying a meal together. And I subsequently delivered them to their home.

About two weeks later, thanks again to Candace, I learned of another special service at Cornerstone and decided I would like to attend, so after a season of prayer, I decided to ask the mother if she and her daughters would like to go as before. She told me that the daughters had previously committed to a swimming event at the apartment of a young lady who also attended Hillcrest Church, but, she continued "I'd like to go."

Well, Cindy and I have discussed these events more than a few times since and have both admitted that, while it was enjoyable, neither of us heard any thunderous fireworks (but perhaps a couple of "sparklers") go off during either of those first two events. And Cindy also made it so very clear that there would not have been a first event had anyone other than the Reverend Derek Prince been the speaker at Cornerstone.

And get this! That was the very last service that Reverend Prince held in the United States. Because of health issues, he returned to his beloved Israel, from which he was subsequently called home to be everlasting with his Lord and Savior.

You may be wondering why this was included. Well, unknown to me, Cindy had been praying and telling the Lord that, if He had someone for her with which she was to share the balance of her life, she wanted Him to send this person to her church (Hillcrest) because she would not go church-hopping to find a Christian mate. And unknown to Cindy, I had been praying to the Lord that, if I were to be married again, I wanted a godly woman whom He handpicked for me since my track record for making important life choices had proven to be far short of stellar.

So Cindy and I began to see each other on an ongoing basis. We learned that each of us had placed Jesus first in our lives, which included consistent prayer and Bible study. We discovered that we both liked long drives on backroads where God's creative handiwork was abundantly evident. We both thoroughly enjoyed barbecued pork ribs and the requisite loaded baked potatoes, visiting unique antique shops and warehouses was mutually celebrated, and we as well joyfully celebrated 10 consecutive annual world-class quilting festivals at George R. Brown Convention Center in Houston, yessiree, I'm an unapologetic throwback. I like quilts!

In short, we had several compatible preferences, which, with heaven's enabling, assured an excellent fit that would assuredly strengthen the expectation of a lifelong relationship. I know with certainty that she is my heaven-sent, Spirit-led, prayer-driven, Word-immersed, earthly treasure. I frequently, sincerely, and accurately comment that I married "way over my head."

On January 26, 2000, while still in Seguin, Hillcrest Church had a visiting evangelist pastor/missionary, Reverend James Fields, who imparted scripture over me, specifically passages from Luke 24:45 and Exodus 35:30–34, declaring that I would have an understanding of the Word and would become a teacher of it. I received the declaration but frankly with some reservation, not because I thought God was unable, rather because my past behavior and achievements seemed obviously deficient and certainly short of the mark.

Have you ever had thoughts like these? Could He really use someone with a track record like mine? And besides that, why should He? We can be assured that ongoing faithfulness to the Great King and the fullness of His time, not ours, will ultimately reveal heaven's answers to these questions and any similar inquiries that you or I might entertain.

# Chapter 3—Traversing
# New and Varied Paths

So you might be wondering what happened between12 October 1967, the date of my military discharge, and my Corpus Christi "road to Damascus" in April 1982? Well, it's now time to return to Sears, Roebuck & Company in San Antonio to resume my career path, make my mark, buy a house, and raise a family, in short, to climb the so-called "ladder of success."

So I flew to New Orleans to pick up the beige 1967 VW beetle that we had bought, paid for, and shipped back to United States, with free shipping courtesy of the US government. We rented an apartment until spring 1968 and then purchased our first home with a $13,750 VA housing loan and a new 1967 Mustang so that we each had adequate, economical, and dependable transportation to our respective jobs.

It was quite obvious that we were now in the mode of realizing the American dream. The relatively few times we attended church was primarily when my mother visited, plus most of the Christmas and Resurrection services. We were so busy making money to accumulate all the stuff. And with few exceptions, when we did attend, it was a pathetic event, as we patted our hands and attempted an uninspired effort at singing while thinking where we might go for lunch and all the things that tomorrow held.

Were we tithing? You've got to be kidding! With mortgage and auto payments and furniture to buy, which brought credit card debt, we convinced ourselves that we needed all of our income to keep our head above water, not to mention our firstborn was coming in August 1969, and we certainly needed to prepare the nursery.

So all of this push and shove continues until we are again blessed with the arrival of our second child in November 1972. Now we just have to buy a larger home with an additional bedroom. And oh yes, a larger vehicle is needed, an economical 1972 Toyota station wagon, along with more new furniture for the dining room and the nursery and, of course, the requisite rocker/recliner. Well, you get the picture.

Employment promotions occur. So why not get a larger house? Plus we can choose colors and determine the interior finish as it is being built. And oh yes, a new vehicle will look great in that spacious new garage. Hey, why not have a carpenter build cabinets on each side of the fireplace and get new stereo speakers and a more powerful stereo receiver? And oh yes, we need a new turntable to play all those LP albums in that large den that we now have. Wow! Why not get new furniture for the formal living-dining area that we almost never use but really needs to consistently look good. Agree?

Tithe? Offering? No, a few token dollars now and then, but we are at least now on semi-regular occasions attending church services for the benefit of our two wonderful daughters, don't you know? More promotions come.. And hey, why not buy a garden home with a rear-entry garage. The larger den will nicely accommodate four speakers for the entertainment system. Quadra-sonic, remember that? There's less grass to mow. After all, we're just so busy these days. Sound familiar?

While the number three has multiple implications in God's economy, I felt that "testing" was an appropriate choice for the title of this third chapter in my life since, in retrospect, it is readily apparent that God was abundantly blessing us. And it now seems quite probable that He was observing where my heart was and how I would choose to steward His favor. And as you have just read, there was so very much yet to be learned.

Does any of this sort of thinking and activity ring true? Be real now. Are we the only ones that did or is doing this? My sincere prayer and expectation is that you will allow the Lord to enable you to vault over the poor choices that are being chronicled herein and at a much earlier age than we did. Please don't duplicate our blatant errors and poor choices. Trust us. They aren't all that.

# Chapter 4—Pondering Termination of Current Habits

Looking back in the rearview mirror has brought a recognition of how I was during my twenties and thirties. I now know that my approach to God was actually a parroting of what I had observed from my mother and other Christ followers. That is, I duplicated what had been demonstrated to me. While I totally agree that it is absolutely essential to "train up a child in the way he should go" (Prov. 22:6), it has finally become equally obvious to me that there must also come a time in the life of every adult individual when a conscious decision is made to develop his or her very own, self-initiated, intimate, and consistent relationship with the Lord.

I recall how I would stand when they stood, sit when they sat, clap when they did (in rhythm with the songs/choruses being sung). It was cold, lifeless religion (form without power) and absolutely not a relationship. It strikes me that males are probably guiltier of this. Perhaps we subconsciously think that outward displays of emotion are more for the ladies and children, or maybe it's the macho male belief that we will appear soft, especially if we should shed tears.

I finally overcame the erroneous belief that men don't cry when I accepted the truth that Jesus wept at the time of Lazarus's death (John 11:35) and over Jerusalem (Luke 19:41). Peter wept bitterly (Matt. 26:75) after his three-time denial of the Lord. Paul shed tears night and day (Acts 20:31). So much for the often-accepted declaration that real men don't cry. I refused to permit the possibility of an ulcerated stomach due to excessively acid-laden internals. selah

I also recall thinking what lunch might bring and thought about what had happened at work yesterday, last week, and last month. I also pondered several impending and dreaded projects yet to be done. And of course, those thoughts concerning the sporting events that were to be televised that day and in the upcoming week, the possibility of playoff opportunity for my favorite teams, and not to mention my bowling prowess and what I might do for improvement in that arena.

Mental distractions were frequent, and my retention of the good news was insufficient. Actually "negligible" would be more accurate. Educators inform us that we forget about 95 percent of what we hear in just seventy-two hours. I think that, with few exceptions, it was more like seventy-two minutes for me. I feel certain that occurred because I was being exposed to considerable kingdom understanding and as Matthew 13:19 reveals, that's the one message that concerns satan so profoundly that he injects himself rather than trusting one of his minions with the assignment . (By the way, I refuse to capitalize satan's name, not because I'm in denial of his existence, but rather because I'm in refusal of his attempts to bully, lie, or deceive. I have chosen to continually think "greater is He who is in me.").

In any event, this hollow lifestyle was totally unfulfilling. It held such little significance. I really felt like I was running in place and going nowhere. Clearly, a life that is lived without a sincere regard for God is reminiscent of the vanity declared in Ecclesiastes 1:2. It is obvious to me now that my greatest problem at that point in my life was spiritual ignorance. Since no spiritual relationship—abiding, intimacy, and presence— had been sought, cultivated, and eventually appropriated to overarch me, there was no source available to me on a constant basis to draw me to the wellspring of spiritual knowledge and the accompanying subsequent and crucial growth.

And because an insignificant investment was being made by me, an equivalent return was being realized, truly a picture-perfect demonstration of reaping what is sown. Please allow me to encourage you to the point of insistence that you refuse to walk through life unfulfilled and powerless due to a failure on your part to access the fullness of the presence of the Holy Spirit. And please, PLEASE, P-L-E-A-S-E don't allow five, ten, twenty, or more years to pass, only to then realize that you have a disappointingly empty—yes, very unproductive—history of grievous dissatisfaction with your then current station in life.

Listen up. If you knew today that five, ten, fifteen, or, for that matter, even just one more year from now, there would be no appreciable increase in satisfaction with the life you are living today, would you entertain an all-out determination to do whatever is needed to assure a different outcome? How many times have you heard it said, "if I had known then what I know now, I would surely have done things differently"? And you may also wish to recall that the definition for insanity has been stated as continuing to do what you've always done and expecting a different result.

Consider this. Just walk around at leisure, at work, or even at church for the next few days or weeks and observe the behavior of folks nearby. Notice how many of them are angry, bored, cynical, detached, hurting, lonely, obviously unfulfilled, pretentious, or, worst of all, hopeless--that state of mind that fully expects that the current set of intolerable circumstances will never change. And should you be currently at this level, you already know full well that hopelessness is not solely specific to persons living in so-called Third World countries.

Or try this. Go to lunch with a group, including a church group, and observe the topics of conversation. Oh, they may have talented children, new cars, big houses, good jobs, nice clothes, and such, but this question continues to cross my mind, "I know, but are you fulfilled?"

Should you feel that I am being somehow unfairly judgmental in my assessment of this condition, please rest assured that I am only relating a set of circumstances with which I am intimately familiar. In short, I've been there and unfortunately done that! How about you? Do you, as you may have heard it said, know all the verses to that song?

The bottom line to all this seems to be, now that I have recognized it and further have freely admitted it, what action am I now ready to pursue to assure a more fulfilling path? Does this perhaps sound like something you should consider as well? I'm just asking. Regarding your present life, how's that working for you? You will surely know when you once again suffer another of those sleepless nights that includes tossing and turning with those nasty pains of unfulfilled emptiness. Don't you just absolutely detest those tortuous occurrences?

Seriously, have you ever thought to yourself something like, "Surely, there just must be more to life than this"? The big question just has to be, "What are you and I willing to do to eliminate such aggravation and awful disappointment?"

I genuinely feel that completion is the most appropriate identifier for this fourth chapter as I was beginning to tire of those many undesirable aspects in my daily struggle and just wanted to bring them to a point of termination. Have you arrived there yet? selah

While the exact meaning of "selah" is uncertain, some biblical scholars and students feel it may mean to pause, ponder, consider, or reflect. Thank you for extending grace to me for using it with that understanding.

# Chapter 5—Recognition
## of Potential Destiny

In late 1967, three of life's great questions struck me. You know the ones. Where did I come from? What is my purpose? Where am I going? A six-month-long world's fair was held in San Antonio, dubbed Hemisfair '68. It actually began in October 1967 and ended in March 1968. Included in the many and varied exhibits was a thought-provoking place named "The Ireland House." It displayed many coats of arms and prompted the thought of the possibility, however remote, that, sometime in history past, I might have had a predecessor who became a person deserving of honor. And hence, just perhaps, I might be entitled to a coat of arms.

Well, this began a jaunt that would drive me into a variety of research, which, unknown to me, would soon become an addictive pursuit that would include the study of American and some British history. Little did I realize that the once-dreaded and boring study of history, with sincere apologies to John Lewis, could develop into a passion that would shortly find me on a trek back to the dawn of time. Hmm, was this yet another Jehovah Sneaky plan?

Jehovah Sneaky is clearly not a name attributed to our Creator in his Holy Word, but rather it's a reverent term of endearment to identify a most gracious Father who is love (1 John 4:8, 16), who planned our destiny and purpose before the foundation of the world, and who desires to be daily involved in enabling us to achieve its available abundance.

In any event, I soon discovered that, in order to learn about my predecessors, it was best to start with myself and work in reverse. So I asked my mother who our oldest living ancestor was, and she led me to my paternal great-aunt Loula (Lulu), who, at age ninety-one, was born well before the advent of the television/electronics era and thus had sufficient time and ample memory space to become the family historian. She confidently and frequently stated that she would live to age one hundred; however, she was incorrect, she actually lived to 103 and 11 months. Her memory was found to be considerable and proved to be both historically and factually accurate again and again. Armed with her input; close contact with other genealogists; an insatiable appetite for numerous trade-related magazines; and considerable facts about my grandparents, great-grandparents, and great-great grandparents, including, but not limited to, walking through many cemeteries (think grass burrs, "goat heads," thorns, and barbed wire fence) in Central and South Texas, Louisiana, and Georgia. I subsequently located a substantial quantity of the Civil War military records pertaining to both of my paternal great-grandfathers by writing to the government record keeping agency known as the Government Services Administration.

And the purpose of all this seemingly disassociated information? I am absolutely convinced that our heavenly Abba Father so loves us that He will formulate a plan so very undetectable and yet, in retrospect, so obviously essential. Do you see it? He knows that, if I become passionate about who I am and from whence I originated, I am likely to follow a path that, if continued, will ultimately lead me directly to the originator, albeit a circuitous and likely lengthy journey.

The discovery and recognition of this inexplicable kind of love literally takes my breath. It serves to so powerfully impress me that it immediately is obvious that, if a God like this will openly display such love (1 John 3:1), it becomes so impossible to determine the incalculable gifts (James 1:17) of love that are not as readily apparent, that is:

- His behind-the-scenes favor (Prov. 12:2a);
- protection from enemy assault (Ps. 91:11);
- the affordance of life in all of its available abundance (John 10:10);
- the direction of my path (Ps. 16:11; Prov. 3:5–6; Acts 2:28);
- the gift of the desires of my heart (John 17:24); and
- His frequent "showing up", His "presence" (James 4:8)

Thus this convinces me that probably 90 percent or more of His love toward me goes undetected by me. I cannot help but wonder. Did the psalmist David have this in mind when he penned, "What is man, that you are mindful (your mind is full?) of him?" (Ps. 8:4, 144:3).

I am confident that one day this question is certain to be answered. I can hardly wait to ask King David about this thought-provoking verse. Do you also have your own list of items to discuss with heaven's Hall of Heroes?

# Chapter 6—Assessment of My Track Record

So let's see now. What events have occurred thus far. I was born. I was dedicated to God. I was trained in the way I should go. I attended school and college. I learned about God. I served in the military. I got married. I began a career. I had progeny. I accumulated stuff. I struggled with depression. I made foolish choices. I suffered a twenty-two-year career loss. I subsequently experienced a twenty-seven-year failed marriage and more of those foolish choices. I lived in my own strength. I leaned upon my own understanding. I became heavily indebted. I suffered an additional career loss. Ad nauseum.

And then finally—and I do mean finally—I found myself amidst the stench on my posterior, peering up from the slime of the putrid, proverbial, prodigal pigsty. Then I eventually "came to myself" and belatedly realized that there just has to be some more desirable solution to all of this fully nauseating emptiness, all of the pretense, all of the plastic, all of the overt phoniness, and all of the incessant searching while attempting to fill the seemingly bottomless void that had so enveloped me for these past forty years. That sounds so very much like the length of an all too familiar Hebrew wilderness trip, huh? Running in circles. Yuck!

About that time, I began to openly verbalize that I had, until this very point in time, clearly only mimicked the heavenly relationship that my mother had so faithfully demonstrated as a lifestyle before me. I had not yet of my own volition even begun to develop a personal, let alone, intimate relationship with my creator. Oh, of course, I was His creation. I knew about Him, but I was not a friend to Him (John 15:14). And this was the primary reason that I quite regularly fell prey to sin and its accompanying deceptive and destructive consequences. I have since learned that, if I fail to continually prAy, I surely will become ongoing prEy.

My astute, excellent, friend and fellow servant of the Great King, the Reverend Earnest Williams, states that an appropriate acrostic for sin is self-inflicted nonsense. I consider that assessment to be absolutely spot on.

When I consider that I am a free moral agent and I choose whether to sin or not ("take every thought captive")(2 Cor. 10:5) and further when I understand that sinning makes no sense as it is clearly designed to steal, kill, and destroy, what further consideration is needed? May I be so bold as to state that it is blatantly apparent that a disturbingly large percentage, if not most, self-proclaimed Christ followers are unfortunately wandering about in essentially this very same predicament? They know about—or perhaps to be more precise—have heard about the one called the Christ, but an intimate and personal relationship with Him is more accurately understood to be relatively nonexistent.

Tolerating this state of anemic condition becomes unmistakably obvious when everyday living deals a harsh blow and the victim of such an attack quickly responds with "What am I going to do?" or even worse "Why is this happening to me?" rather than intimately and intensely discussing the matter via the vehicle of prayer with the one with whom they claim to be a devotee and subsequently entrusting Him with the final flawless outcome.

For my part, it seems so very clear that I had missed the full import of Jesus's poignant declaration, "I am the door"

(John 10:7–9). I finally came to understand that a pastor, teacher, or other person could guarantee me that an even greater life after my rebirth is achievable, but to attain it requires my personal determination to fully pursue an ongoing, intimate, Spirit-led relationship with the Lord.

In short, Jesus paid the price for my salvation, but I am required to pay the price for my commitment. And should I choose not to pursue, I can rest assured that an experience of a lack of fulfillment is on my spiritual horizon and the very likely probability that I will also regress due to my spiritual inactivity.

That daunting realization has so impacted me when I now consider that, if He is the door, it seems clear that there must also be something beyond the door of salvation that can only be accessed through Him. After all, the purpose of a door is to move from one reality to another, correct? So now that this recognition has sufficiently impacted me, what steps am I both willing and fully determined to take so a needed turnabout can occur that will positively lead to the desired target, that is, my God-ordained destiny? What then is one to do? Am I to think, ponder, pause, muse, meditate, reflect, consider, ruminate, or perhaps even repent? Hmm, what a radical concept, the metamorphosis (renewing) of my mind (Rom. 12:2).

*The Big Question:*

*If you don't choose to spend your days pursuing Jesus in this relatively short lifetime, why would you want to be with Him forever?*

My, my, my, just think of that. Did you get that? It's not simply changing my mind. No, it's the renewing of my mind, thinking in an entirely different way. Perhaps it is best stated as I refuse to think as I used to think. This obviously takes

Holy Spirit-enabling, my determination must become, "I won't leave home without Him!"

As for me, I have made a conscious decision to go well beyond the door of salvation and follow the path into total exploration of the kingdom of heaven that Jesus clearly made the pivotal issue of his three-and-a-half-year ministry on earth and subsequently continued to declare for the forty-day period (Acts 1:1-3) following his resurrection. He then saw to it that, in addition to His library of sixty-six books (the Bible), we would have a spirit guide to lead us into all truth. Yes, the person of the Holy Spirit not only guides us, but Romans 8:26 is an ongoing reminder that He also makes intercession for us with "groanings" that are not to be understood.

What an extravagantly wonderful prayer partner, and when I further recall also that Jesus ever lives to make intercession for me (Heb. 7:25) and continuing further, that I am to pray without ceasing (1 Thess. 5:17), I am then immediately reminded of the truth that a threefold cord is not quickly broken (Eccl. 4:12). Oh, how that must give great consternation to the accuser of the brethren. And that impacting realization fills me with uncontrollable joy.

# Chapter 7--Thankful But Not Satisfied

So it is now April 1982. I'm soon to be forty-one years of age and finally fully capable of an external admission of genuine dissatisfaction with my failure to achieve any substantial growth toward the destiny that God had deposited within and to which I strongly aspired. And that realization is now profoundly impacting me. It isn't as though nothing has been done. There is a foundation. It's just that it seems as though a plateau has been reached and this plateau is only very slightly above the level of the foundation.

This realization is so unacceptable to me. I know I am unwilling to settle for this as a final destination. This state brings to mind a condition you might have observed, those who have accepted Christ and the accompanying Holy Spirit but have relegated the Holy Spirit to the guest room until He is summoned rather than extending refrigerator rights (total and unrestricted access) to Him. This action would seem certain to grieve the Holy Spirit and would as such eliminate any likelihood of producing a fruit-filled life of supernatural abundance.

At this point, I begin to recognize that, in order to attain a higher level, I must review what has been done to arrive at my present state. Only then, after determining where I am, can I begin to formulate what is yet to be done. So as a result of the epiphany while on the road to Corpus Christi and the resultant change, I determined to begin to read through the

Bible each year with the use of the Bible Pathway Devotional. I then recalled that reading approximately fifteen minutes per day could get me through the entire Bible in one year. Additionally the devotional provides a daily list of prayer targets to include the leaders of the governments of the United States and the nations of the world, as directed by the apostle Paul in 1 Timothy 2:1–2.

Let's refresh Paul's exhortation, shall we? "I exhort therefore, that FIRST(caps are mine) of all, supplications, prayers, intercessions, and giving of thanks, be made for all men, for kings, and for all that are in authority, that we may lead a quiet and peaceable life in all godliness and honesty."

This approach eventually broadened my prayer scope from mostly personal petition to communion. The Jesus who lives in me is that common union with heaven, achieved through an everyday quiet time communication. And the subsequent growth ultimately leads to prayers of intercession that are certain to proceed toward developing real concern for the masses. "I have compassion on the multitude" (Mark 8:2) surely sounds like an accurate assessment of Jesus's ministry in just six words.

This daily trek through God's Word also began to impregnate me with much improved memorization of scripture and a greater grasp of what He is all about and where He desires to take every person who hungers to follow His leading, that is,both willing to hear and to live the lifestyle that He both taught and demonstrated.

Additionally I determined to pursue an in-depth Bible study by Dick Eastman entitled "The University of the Word," (Change The World Ministries) which effected a greater immersion in the inestimable delights and further understanding of God's Word.

Warning: If you determine to be consistently and reverentially in the Word, you will discover that it will create a renaissance (Isaiah 43:19)—a new birth within you, not a rehash of the former things—because the words are spirit and they are life (John 6:63). And what a glorious transformation that is certain to effect!

A simultaneous and somewhat parallel vehicle of travel began with Christian television programs and a subsequent sorting out of the attendant teachers and ministers with a desire to determine which of them are on the leading edge of what heaven is directing at any given present moment, and for me, that translates to two crucial issues:

1.  They must be consistently in the Word of God.
2.  They must be continuously entertaining the presence of God (John 5:19, 30; 8:26–29; 12:49–50). After all, that was Jesus's continuous practice.

That is, they can, as every single one of us can, know what He is saying and doing at any given moment. I didn't say it was easily done, but what worthwhile thing is? For example, which do you appreciate most, a potato that is rapidly cooked in a microwave, one that is slowly baked in an oven, or, for that matter, one that is twice-baked?

For my part, an ongoing, determined intimate approach is absolutely essential to avoid being out of both His timing and His will in the right now. Let's just think this through for a moment. Which of our earthly friends is most likely to share his or her choicest and most intimate secrets with us: one we hang out with on an ongoing basis or one with which we have fellowship with every six months or perhaps even less frequently? And since we are made in His likeness (Gen. 1:26-28), isn't it permissible for us to presume that the Lord whose Word declares "draw near to God and he will draw near to you" (James 4:8) and who stands at the door and knocks (seeking entry)(Rev. 3:20) will choose to reveal Himself to those who are determined to rarely find themselves more than a few spiritual heartbeats from his indescribable presence?

While I may be unable to fully tell how consistently these expositors are in His Word and hosting His presence, I can get a strong sense of the importance of these two factors to them as I experience the content of their teaching, their preaching, and their conversation ("for out of the abundance of the heart the mouth speaks".)(Matt. 12:34).

For example, do they spend more time talking of the past events of the Great Awakening, Azusa Street, the great revivals of bygone eras, Charles Haddon Spurgeon, Smith Wigglesworth, Charles Finney, and such, as well as how wonderful the future "sweet bye and bye" is going to be with little or no consistent equipping for the "dreadful here and now"?

And further, if they fail to tell me what I am to do to continually grow the spiritual kingdom of God here on earth ("Do business till I come")(Luke 19:13) and to make disciples of all nations (Matt. 28:19), then I have no interest in their agenda. And to take it a step further, I have absolute disregard for the agenda of those who are the so-called "seeker friendly," i.e.don't hurt their feelings by confronting the sin habits in their life.

Acts 17:26 seems to be supportive of this since my times and residences were chosen and foreknown by the creator of the universe. I doubt that rewards or judgment will accrue to me for the bygone eras that preceded me. Thus it seems certain that my responsibility to Abba Father (Mark 14:36) during my earthly tenure is to appropriately steward the time, talent, and treasure afforded to me so I can become a conduit through which the greatest growth possible can occur in the kingdom of God and, therefore, through the boldness prompted by the enabling power (*dunamis*, Greek) of the Holy Spirit to thus be guided to accomplish and eventually be permitted to echo the statement made by Jesus as recorded in John 17:4, "I have glorified you on the earth, I have finished the work which you have given me (Mike Rogers) to do." I strongly encourage you to choose to insert your name here!

Armed with this reality and responsibility, I began to come to grips with the certainty that an immense quantity of spiritual knowledge must necessarily be garnered and an equivalent amount of godly wisdom is to be acquired in order to have any likelihood of success in accomplishing this tremendous undertaking. So I determined that the best path to follow is to develop an ongoing, personal, and, yes, even an abiding intimate relationship with the God of Proverbs 3, Isaiah 55, the Four Gospels (especially John chapters 5, and 14 through 17), Romans 8, Acts chapters 2 through 4, Revelation 3:20, and many other cornerstone passages. It seems to be a no-brainer to this small town lad now that I have both realized and even more importantly am fully appreciating the certainty that I surely become like those with whom I choose to associate or hang out with.

As mentioned previously, Jesus corroborates this approach when He states clearly that He only says and does what He hears and sees the Father saying and doing. And who knows the Father and what He desires better than Jesus? So the thought occurs to me to see, if the Father has demonstrated a desire for this sort of intimacy in times past and since it is certainly a good idea to ultimately arrive at the beginning, Genesis would seem to be the logical place to start.

In Genesis 1:28-30, God gives dominion authority to Adam. In Genesis 2:15, He gives specific direction to Adam, and in Genesis 3:8 and following, God is recorded as walking in the garden in the cool of the day and having dialogue with both Adam and Eve. This feels like a relationship to me.

In Genesis chapters 6 through 8, God verbally guides Noah through the flood. In Genesis 9:8, God addresses Noah and his sons, equating to more relationship. Moving on to Genesis 12, there is God with Abram promising to him unending blessing, and Genesis 15 reveals dialogue, a continuing relationship. In Genesis 18, there is Abraham and Sarah. God renamed both Abram and Sarai. There is Isaac in Genesis 26 and Jacob in Genesis 28, 32, and 35. Of course there is Moses in Exodus 3:3-4. And please do not miss the poignant fact that, when Moses turned aside from the mundane activity of sheepherding to see what God was up to, God showed up at once (Ex. 3:4) and talked to him.

God, through the person of the Holy Spirit, still shows up even today. If you haven't done so recently or if you have never done so, try this out for yourself. Say something intentional like, "Father, I am so hungry for you that I am now going to separate myself from all electronic and human distractions and turn aside and bare my heart fully to you. And further, I am committed to remain here until I have completely experienced your indescribable and matchless presence."

Be forewarned, if you attempt this in full sincerity with a pure and tender heart filled with love and emptied of all previous unforgiveness and holding nothing back and are in a state of total expectation, a discernible sense of His overwhelming presence will prevail. You can rest assured of it. Right now would be a wonderful time for you to experience that extravagant gift. Go ahead. I will joyfully await your return.

Welcome back! Okay, so in the present New Testament era, does He still seek relationship? After all, there are surely a lot more people on earth at this much later time in history. Immediately there comes to mind how he mentored twelve tough guys.

Perhaps rogues is a better description since one used profanity in the process of denying Him three times and two wanted to call down fire from heaven to destroy others who were also in ministry, but just not in the same circle. Another was one of those despised tax collectors that sold out to the

Romans. Yet another doubted Him, and of course, there was the one who stole from the money bag and ultimately sold Him out.

And despite all of those shortcomings, He lovingly chose to eat, sleep, walk, talk, encourage, abide their stinky feet and breath, redirect, and display lifestyle to them for three and a half years. Without a doubt, it seems like fellowship, relationship, and intimacy, especially when you consider that He never gave up on even one of them.

But what about after His death and burial when they were all hiding out and were fear-filled and doubting, in spite of the fact that some of His closest acquaintances reported having seen Him resurrected? Would He still want intimate relationship with them? Acts 1 and First Corinthians 15:1-8 reveal that Jesus returned to fellowship with His followers, as many as five hundred-plus at one time, for a full forty days and continued to teach His only message, that is, the kingdom of God (Luke 4:43, 16:16).

And we dare not forget Saul of Tarsus who was actively involved in the persecution, incarceration, and death of the saints and how Jesus talked with him on the road to Damascus, with Paul later stating that he received his personal assignment through the revelation of Jesus and not from other men (Acts 20:24-25; Gal. 1:6-12). Not even Gamaliel, who was probably the finest teacher of the law during that period in history (Acts 5:34, 22:3). And no, not even from Christ's apostles. It pretty much reduces it to intimate spiritual relationship, doesn't it?

So since God's Son, the greatest teacher who ever lived and the one who personally loved and knew Jehovah God eternally, thought it essential to consistently only do and say what He observed the Father doing and saying, how dare I even consider taking any different approach, especially when being told that the wondrous works that He did would be done and greater than these (John 14:12-14).

45

Hmm, thus it seems patently obvious that, in order to attain such seemingly unlikely results, Jesus's methods are the ones to emulate if such incalculably wonderful works are to come to fruition. You perhaps have heard it said that some people are so heavenly minded that they are no earthly good. It seems quite obvious that Jesus's lifestyle disproves such a result; rather if we are genuinely heavenly minded, we only do and say what we see the Father doing and saying. And such action obviously cannot result in no earthly good since it is clearly the Father's will. Are we able to reach agreement on this line of thinking?

So at this stage of my life, it becomes obvious that there had to be some stimulus that resulted in a conscious decision being made by me "to refuse to be who I used to be" and that included the determination that the fear of man (Heb. 13:6) would no longer throttle my inner drive for spiritual boldness. So just how did this desire for a new higher level of spiritual relationship reveal itself?

As is often the case with God's plan, it wasn't all that obvious at the outset. It began with a Sunday-by-Sunday human request, and ultimately after several weeks of request, it became more of an insistence that we should begin a weekly Bible study (care group) at the home of a couple we will identify as Mike and Rachel. This persistence subsequently led to a starting date of April 2, 2010 (Good Friday). And no, we did not intentionally choose this holy day. We actually came to realize it much later. Was this one of those so-called Holy Spirit-directed appointments?

As study began for this adventure, it quickly became evident that heaven had a higher purpose in mind than just a weekly gathering with a few verses, some fellowship (including food and Rachel's world class salsa), a bit of prayer, a handful of choruses with that guitar, and dismissal after an hour or so. No, the architect of this plan breathed specific scripture and direction that was to be followed to achieve the desired result. The Holy Spirit made it quite clear that this absolutely would not be a microwave event where participants might expect a turnabout in a matter of minutes, hours, weeks, months, or even a year or so. No, it became so obvious that this plan would both develop and bring maturity one day at a time, one step at a time, for a lifetime, or until Jesus's return. This definitely was not an assignment for the lazy, the half-hearted, the fearful, or sissies or pretenders, although some might have started in one of those categories. The very first scripture "breathed" was Romans 12:1-2.

A quick study of the Greek language for "renewing" required my acceptance of the certainty that a metamorphosis of my mind—and how can I teach this if I'm not intentionally in the process of personally applying this—was so absolutely essential in order for me to move from the status of a worm (caterpillar) into a cocoon where an extensive, intensive, unfamiliar, not to mention quite uncomfortable, renovation was necessary to, "in the fullness of time," result into the eventual creation of a "beautiful butterfly."

This was such an obvious indicator that an ongoing and lengthy journey lay ahead. The good news that followed gave the confidence that resting in the Father's presence and abiding in his logos assured that the desired results (His customized plan for the destiny of each determined attendee) were achievable, indeed the certainty of path direction for all those who trust in the Lord (Ps. 16:11; Prov. 3:5-6) and the assurance that all things can be achieved by those who fully trust in the source of strength provided through Christ (Phil. 4:13).

All of this is coupled with the prescription ("Rx" means recipe) to avoid deception as spelled out by the daily reading of the Word (the method employed by both the Jews and Greeks in Berea)(Acts 17:11b); a worker who does not need to be ashamed, rightly dividing the word of truth" (2 Tim. 2:15); and the knowledge that all scripture is inspired (God-breathed) and profitable for thorough equipping for every good work (2 Tim. 3:16-17) with each of these verses bringing additional depth, direction, and synergistic impact to the promise of the Holy Spirit. All of this brought the assurance that it is indeed possible for every so-called average human being to achieve spiritual success in the kingdom of God far beyond what his or her previous understanding or belief might have been.

A favorite kingdom growth parable of mine contains the fewest words. It's thirty-three words in Luke 13:20–21 and twenty-nine words in Matthew 13:33, both NKJV. But perhaps it is the most poignant, "And again He (Jesus) said, 'To what shall I liken the kingdom of God? It is like leaven (yeast) which a woman took and hid in three measures of meal until all was leavened.'"

Let's dissect this. We have a typical woman in an humble setting performing a seemingly menial task, and yet Jesus likens that to the kingdom of God? Really? Well, we know that Jesus had previously likened leaven to teaching when speaking of the Pharisees and Herod (Mark 8:15). We also know that leaven is not visually observable once added to the meal; however, the greatest result is yet to come, "in the fullness of time" when the yeast doubles or triples its initial volume.

We further know that great growth is exactly what Jesus referred to when we review the context provided in the parable immediately preceding this, that is, the tiny mustard seed that grew to become an herb tree under whose limbs the birds may find shade. We then need only to read Jesus's assessment of John the Baptist and the comparison of John to the least person in the kingdom of God (Matt. 11:11; Luke 7:28) as well as Jesus's promise that the works that He (Jesus) did, His followers would do and greater than those because He would go to the Father.

And just in case you feel certain that signs, wonders, and miracles ceased with the passing of Jesus's apostles, please consider this. Do you seriously believe that God who has declared the end from the beginning (Isa. 46:10), who is also no respecter of persons (Acts 10:34), and whose very essence is love (1 John 4:8,16) would actually cause a cessation of such wondrous activity and, in effect, abandon all of humanity that was to follow to be subject to the savage hatred and treacherous deeds of the evil one (for example, AIDS, cancer, carpal tunnel syndrome, diabetes, Legionnaires' disease, Ebola, poliomyelitis, PTSD, fibromyalgia, STDs, and on and on). Especially after recalling Psalm 78:11, 32, 43 and Psalm 106:13, 21-22, God clearly was angry because Israel continued to forget His works, which then invariably resulted in Israel falling into the depths of idolatry every single time. Are you listening America? Not to mention Jesus's own words as recorded in John 14:10-14.

And then continuing to push even further, may I very respectfully ask how many persons you know or, for that matter, have you even heard about that demonstrate such confidence in the Lord that they consistently walk in expectation of Christ-demonstrated signs, miracles, wonders, and works as they are led by the person of the Holy Spirit?

And may I further ask you to consider this extremely uncomfortable question? If those who do not yet know Christ as their personal Savior can take their choice of many Christian denominations to learn how to come into a saving relationship with Jesus Christ, why in the world should they even consider your house of worship if they are unable to see an observable and desirable difference between yours and the many other choices?

And now that I have weighed that truth in my spirit, I hear the question resounding in my soul. Am I one of those rare persons? And if I am not, what am I both willing and determined to do with Holy Spirit enablement so I can become such a one?

I am learning that this supernatural expectation can occur only after an individual begins to walk in "the God kind of faith" as demonstrated in Genesis 1:3 and following when God makes several declarations, including "Let there be light" and followed shortly by the phrase of fulfillment, "and it was so." And Genesis 1:7, 9, 11, 15, 24, 30 continue to declare the fulfillment of additional declarations.

Perhaps you believe that this demonstration of godly faith occurred only during the six days of original creation. Would you please recall that, while on earth, Jesus had chosen to set aside His godly advantages to demonstrate to us that, as believers with His human level of godly faith, great works, signs, and wonders were available?

As one such example, consider the New Testament creative miracle where Christ formed eyeballs of clay. Remember that John 1:3 and Colossians 1:16-17 proclaim that all things were made through Him (which would include that very clay), spit on them (which scientists now tell us that the purest form of DNA comes from inside the mouth, and I'm very certain that Jesus already knew that fact), and placed them in the empty sockets. And the recipient received his sight. (John 9:6-7)

Or consider the declaration that Jesus made over the barren fig tree and the results as recorded in Mark 11:11–24 and the amazing statement made by the Lord in Mark 9:23, "If you can believe, ALL THINGS are possible to him who believes" And how about the bold declaration made by Peter at the gate Beautiful in Acts 3 and the accompanying miracle? And then please revisit the reaction of the spectators as recorded in verses 10 and 11 of Acts chapter three, all the people ran together...greatly amazed...they were filled with wonder and amazement at what had happened. selah

Just how many of this kind of miracle do you think would be necessary in order to fill your small group, your sanctuary, or, for that matter, the largest sports arena in your community when you recall the promise that, in Jesus's name, signs of demon eviction, healing, protection from deadly drinks and poisonous serpents, and the speaking of a heaven-inspired language would follow those who believe (Mark 16:17-18, 20)?

The bottom line is that nothing happens in the kingdom of God until a declaration is made (2 Cor. 4:13-15) by a person who is in right relationship with the Lord Jesus Christ and has the "God kind of faith" as stated in Mark 11:22. We need to understand that the translation of "have faith in God" in literal Greek translation directly converts in English to "have the God kind of faith." It sort of has the ring of calling those things that be not as though they were (Rom. 4:17) or perhaps calling kingdom of heaven activity into our earthly realm, which sounds a lot like "thy kingdom come, thy will be done ON EARTH just as it is in heaven."

But here is where the really tough choice occurs. As previously stated, insanity has been said to be defined as continuing to do what you've always done but expecting a different result. I readily admit that I experienced conviction when first I heard that definition of insanity. And I did not relish tossing it in here, but since I refuse to be who I used to be, I am required to do so because the Holy Spirit has quite clearly impressed me that I must not teach, encourage, or exhort others to take difficult steps or make uncomfortable changes if I am not in the process of doing so myself. You know that routine. It's the old, worn-out cliché, "Don't do as I do, do as I say", ruse. The Holy Spirit has made it profoundly clear that I am to consistently make my lifestyle a relentless, observable, conscious pursuit, implementation, and teaching of biblical truths with Christ-led motives or be fully prepared to be taken to the spiritual woodshed for firm redirection.

Which of us enjoys those encounters? In short, I had better not be guilty of either pretending or part-timing. If I am not truly doing my Spirit-guided, level best to display a lifestyle that releases the power-filled essence of the person of the Holy Spirit as I walk out my daily assignment without regard for my physical surroundings—whether at work; In the mall, grocery store, gas station, or sporting event; or while hunting, fishing, camping, playing, exercising, or dare I mention, parenting? Or for that matter, you name it. "Go ye into all the world" carries with it the implication of "and as you are going" or, in the vernacular of today, whatever I am doing. In short, it is to be a lifestyle. It's who I am! It's what I do!

So would you be willing to consider the following to be an appropriate acrostic for a Holy Spirit-led LIFESTYLE:

**L**oving
**I**ntimate
**F**ellowship
**E**nough
**S**o
**T**hat
**Y**ehovah (or Yeshua)
**L**eads
**E**verything

It has very much of a Proverbs 3:5-6 ring to it, doesn't it? It removes all the pressure caused by the concerns of decision making. We can entrust them to our heavenly Father, the same one who is love. What a wonderful advantage, agree?

On another occasion while in preparation for the Friday night care group gathering, the Holy Spirit dropped the following into my spirit for consideration. Could the Bible be called "God's resume'? After all, just like a job resume', it declares:

1. His name ("I am")(Ex. 3:14)
2. His address ("Heaven is my throne")(Isa. 66:1)

3. His contact information ("Call unto me and I will answer"(Jer. 33:3)
4. His work history ("In the beginning God created") (Gen 1:1; John 5:17)
5. His results ("I do what I say I will do")(1 Kings 8:56; Isa. 55:11)
6. His availability ("I will never leave you nor forsake you") (Heb. 13:5b)
7. His capabilities (omnipotence, omniscience, and omnipresence)
8. His future (eternal)(Eph. 3:9-11)

So after having read His entire resume' from Genesis 1:1 to Revelation 22:21, I then have a decision to make. Will I decide to simply file His resume' with all the others in my filing cabinet, or will I choose to avail myself of His incomparable abilities and provision for all of my everlasting life? Additionally, will I choose to employ Him as a part-timer, which means relegating Him to the guest room and telling Him to wait there until I call for Him, which is certain to be only when I am in need or in trouble? Or will I select Him as a full-timer and afford Him refrigerator rights, which includes granting Him full access to every room in the house, while remembering that my body is the temple that houses the Holy Spirit? And will I develop an ongoing intimate relationship in which I make a conscious decision to commune with Him as my best friend throughout each day?

May I interject here that this is what is inarguably necessary in order to make Jesus my Lord and not just my Savior? Please, may I be allowed to ask you to seriously consider the incontrovertible necessity of taking this action for yourself. For my part, it is absolute certainty that this action is the determining factor between just knowing ABOUT Jesus as opposed to actually knowing Him. Consider this: If Jesus the perfect Son of God found it necessary to only do and say what He saw and heard the Father doing and saying (John 5:19,30, 8:28b–29, 12:49–50), how can I possibly deceive myself by thinking that there is some shortcut to be taken that will permit me to employ a part-time relationship with Him?

Hence, this recognition requires that I must, like Jesus, develop and continuously grow the habit of spending daily quiet time with heaven through the leadership of the person of the Holy Spirit (John 16:13–15). This is not negotiable, and it is not simply some flippant thirty-second or two-minute prayer that is squeezed in sometime during the day, time permitting. No this is a daily, set-aside appointment that I am determined to make the first priority in my schedule. In Matthew 6:33 Jesus words are, "But seek first the kingdom of God and His righteousness." Please notice that it doesn't say "second," "third," or "when I get around to it."

Consider the following scripture as further confirmation of the necessity of this habit. How about Matthew 4:4 (KJV), "Man shall not live by bread alone, but by every word that proceedeth out of the mouth of God." Please note that the tense of the word proceedeth conveys the meaning what God is saying right now. In English, we know it as the present perfect tense so, in order to be in tune with what God is doing at any given moment, doesn't it follow that we are to be in step with Him at every given moment?

One more time, please recall the following: Jesus only did what He saw the Father doing. So let's review some of His various methods of healing as examples:

- Luke 8:43–44 reports that the woman with the issue of blood touched the hem of Jesus's robe and was immediately healed. Note that she touched; He did not.
- Then in Acts 8 verses 54–55, Jesus raises Jairus's daughter when He took her by the hand and told

her to arise. In this instance, He both touched and commanded.

- In Matthew 9:1–8, Jesus healed a paralyzed man (Matt. 9:6b) by words alone, no touch.
- In Matthew chapter 9 verses 27–30, two blind men received sight through His touch and their faith.
- Jesus healed the dying son of a nobleman (John 4:46–53) by the spoken Word and the faith of the nobleman (John 4:50b). This event occurred while Jesus was in Cana of Galilee and the son was at the point of death some sixteen miles away in the city of Capernaum, thereby fully confirming that distance is of no concern when operating in the realm of the Great King.

And hence, knowing that Jesus only did/said what He saw the Father doing/saying, isn't it clearly obvious that none of us should ever consider operating in a different manner? And to be able to walk in alignment with this demonstration of varying techniques would seem to be achievable only by being totally and continuously attuned to heaven, which seems reminiscent of, and likely related to, a mind that is "stayed on thee" (Isa. 26:3b).

And while Jesus demonstrated the fact that various types of methods are used to accomplish physical healing, it would seem reasonable to consider that spiritual healing would also be achieved through multiple avenues, further substantiating the necessity of being in constant communication with the source of every good and every perfect gift (James 1:17).

Perhaps you are thinking something like, "I have so many things to accomplish daily, and it is not humanly possible to devote such extravagant quantities of time and still fulfill my earthly responsibilities." Then should we perhaps consider removing some scripture from our Bible, such as:

- "I can do all things through Christ who strengthens me" (Phil. 4:13).
- "If you can believe, all things are possible to him who believes" (Mark 9:23).
- "But we have the mind of Christ" (1 Cor. 2:16b).
- "Pray without ceasing" (1 Thess. 5:17).
- "And whatever things you ask in prayer, believing, you will receive." (Matt. 21:22).

Of course not. Instead please consider this. Wouldn't it be far better to return to the exhortation in Romans 12:2 that instructs me not to be conformed to or "shoved into the mold of this world," a harsh term? But rather I should be transformed by the renewing of my mind so that a demonstration of what is the good, acceptable, and perfect will of God can be brought into existence? And to fully appreciate the profound significance of this transformation, we must understand that the exact same word (Strong's 3339) used for transformed in Romans 12:2 was also used in Matthew 17:2 and Mark 9:2 when Jesus was transfigured, and as well by Paul in 2 Corinthians 3:18 when speaking of the glory of the new covenant.

Oh yes, it absolutely does require a difficult and sizable change in my thought process (repentance) and a brand-new renaissance of thinking. Undoubtedly it necessitates unlearning some incorrect thought patterns. But isn't this new thought path inarguably essential if even a remote possibility exists that I could do the works that Jesus did and even greater works than those (John 14:12–14). Does this realization strike you as profoundly in your level of faith as it has me? I feel certain that I cannot be alone in this awestruck state.

Another such test of my faith level occurs when revisiting those very honoring words spoken by Jesus concerning John the Baptist as recorded in Luke 7:28, "There is not a greater prophet than John the Baptist." And if that were not enough, He then proceeds to further increase the level of ministry achievable by every kingdom of God participant once the fulfillment of the Lord's promise of the Holy Spirit occurs (Acts 1:8) by continuing with these shocking words of revelation, "But he that is least in the kingdom of God is greater than he."

Friends, I have to tell you honestly, after such a declaration by the King of Kings, I am immediately reminded of—and convicted by is actually more accurate—the honest-hearted comment made by the father of the boy with the unclean (dumb) spirit as recorded in Mark 9:24, "Lord I believe; help my unbelief."

There is no alternative in this matter, it is available to and expected of every resident in the kingdom of God that we not only know the words listed in Mark 9:23, 11:22b–24, 16:16–18, 20 and Matthew 21:21–22. Rather it is essential that we walk them out, that is, they become our lifestyle. Mental assent is simply not sufficient to the task at hand. Assuredly, the Holy Spirit empowerment of Acts 1:8 is required. After all, these are Jesus's words, and yet again we must recall that He only said what He heard the Father saying (John 12:49). This fact alone assures that this is God's will, does it not?

And now that a Spirit-directed and Bible-reinforced renewing of my mind is underway, it doubtless must continue via an ongoing relational growth. This increase in spiritual intimacy will ultimately lead to my recognition, acceptance, and certainly the implementation of, the correct and required approach that will catapult the Christ-led church-at-large into a twenty-first-century kingdom of God explosive-expansion that is certain to become an ongoing display of Acts 2 and beyond.

Further, I know that, in the original document of the book of Acts, there is no mark indicating the end of that book, which would seem to be a certainty that it is an ongoing work leading to the certain fulfillment of Matthew 24:14. So am I now both ready and willing to follow the Lord's example and, to the very best of my ability, preach, teach, share, and demonstrate the lifestyle and message that He so clearly exemplified during His earthly tenure? Since having made a conscious decision of refusing to be who I used to be—perhaps referred to as "stinking thinking"—isn't it probable that He might use the avenues of "rhema" word (what God is saying at any right now moment), divine orchestrated appointment, and Holy Spirit-initiated dreams and visions as methods to direct my every step so that my God-ordained destiny will be fulfilled? After all, there are more than a few instances where God appeared to mankind in dreams and visions and, as previously mentioned, chose to communicate with both women and men. And realizing that He is no respecter of person (Acts 10:34-35) is so powerfully reassuring that I could qualify to be a recipient of these kinds of favor.

Further, since Jesus made it clear that the works that He did could be done by His faith-filled followers, it seems certain that an undaunted, incessant expectation of signs, wonders, and miracles would clearly be forthcoming. And because I am determined to be among those who positively impact the ever-increasing and rapid growth of the kingdom of God, I fully intend to consistently demonstrate a no-holds-barred pursuit of the first covenant promise as recorded in Amos 3:7, "Surely the Lord God does nothing (no thing?) unless He reveals His secret to His servants the prophets".

Well, if he that is least in the kingdom of God is greater than John the Baptist and there is no greater prophet than John, I can see no reason why we should be shy about leading an absolute, all-out frontal assault on the kingdom of darkness by knowing that every promise our Lord has made about the kingdom of God to be both true and therefore achievable, especially if we are fully determined to consistently walk out a Holy Spirit-enabled lifestyle. You will recall that acrostic previously: Loving Intimate Fellowship Enough So That Yeshua Leads Everything.

I am so fully convinced that this is the fact that, in chapter 8, there will be a representative list of signs, wonders, miracles, divine appointments, deliverance, and dreams of which the Lord has graciously allowed my wife and me to be a part through prayer, as eyewitnesses in some cases, and as an ear-witness in one case.

Allow me to preface these events with some assurances:

1. Every one of them is listed for the sole purpose to glorify God.
2. Every one of them occurred after my faith grew well beyond what I had previously thought likely. Rest assured that I had always believed that all things are possible with God. I simply wasn't sure He would choose to use someone with my history.
3. I both revere and fear God far too much to intentionally fabricate or exaggerate any of the information that will follow.

One additional reminder is that God is no respecter of person, which should greatly encourage every individual who reads this testimony to have complete confidence that, as long as you are walking in right relationship with Jesus of Nazareth (lately of heaven), you can fully expect that there are some wonderful, previously planned, heaven-initiated, customized just for you, assignments that are just waiting for you to verbalize your insatiable desire to be used by Him in every single opportunity that He has specifically chosen for you. And you may rest assured, He will never set you up to fail. Simply recall that you can do all things through Christ who is the source of your strength. When you receive any assignment, consider prefacing it with "Here we go, Holy Spirit," as this assures that you have all of the resources of heaven at your disposal. Since you are a representative of heaven on earth (Gen. 1:26–28), you have just given permission for the Father, Son, and Holy Spirit to intervene as needed in earthly affairs.

And further, upon arising each morning, consider asking heaven, "What is/are my assignment(s) today?" However, also consider this caution. Don't ask for an assignment if you aren't sincere because you will receive one (or more) and it (they) almost always come at an inconvenient time, for example, an interruption of your work, lunch, or coffee break by a person(s) or a telephone call, and so on.

Just revisit this sequence of events related by Matthew 9:18–33 how Jesus, while en route to raise Jairus's daughter, had His garment touched by the woman with the ongoing twelve-year flow of blood as He walked along the road, next how the blind men cried out (shouted in desperation) to Him to restore their sight, and finally the demon-possessed mute who was brought to Him. The point being, if the Master willingly experiences interruptions, His servants should fully expect them!

The most important thing to consider is: what action will I take when interruption occurs? Will I recognize that any roadblock is of the enemy and press on in faith, expecting a heaven-driven resolution? Or will the interruption become my excuse? Or equally as unacceptable, will I fail to recognize this as a God moment and thus be unresponsive to the leading of Holy Spirit?

For my part, this should be the time to recall two very important facts:

1. God will make a way where there seems to be no way.
2. There are no coincidences in the life of every genuine Christ follower, "The steps of a good man are ordered by the Lord" (Ps. 37:23).

Knowing that Jesus treated interruptions as opportunities, I must do the same. Please feel free to join me. Or consider following Jesus's directions in Mark 6:7, get yourself a partner and go out by twos. There's absolutely always room for another!

As the completion of this chapter has now arrived, I want to assure you that I in no way want to leave you with the impression that I believe that all knowledge and wisdom has been deposited within me. Rather I just wish to establish that the recognition, acceptance, and, most importantly, the activation of truths whispered to me by the Holy Spirit and the living Words of God (John 6:63) are now being allowed to operate on an ongoing basis and to assure you that I am fully receptive to the truths and events that are assuredly on my spiritual horizon, several of which are to immediately follow.

And please know that I have prayed that every one of you will achieve the fullness of the destiny that God determined for you before the foundation of the world because each of us is needed to bring about the fulfillment of Jesus's words as recorded in Matthew 24:14, "And this gospel of the kingdom will be preached in all the world as a witness to all the nations, and then the end will come."

Please recognize that this scripture unequivocally reveals that it will not be a world catastrophe, weather event, or government collapse; nor will it be the failure of the world monetary system. It will not be a New World Order that brings about the return of our King of Kings. No, it is absolutely crystal clear that the return of the Great King is dependent only upon Jesus's servants delivering His message of the gospel of the kingdom to all nations. And then the end will come.

We must remember that Jesus began His ministry (Matt. 4:17) with the proclamation of the kingdom and continued to preach it throughout his three and a half years on earth. (There are more than one hundred references to the kingdom in the Four Gospels alone.) Then He preached it for forty days after His resurrection (Acts 1:3). And if that were not enough, the apostle Paul preached the kingdom message throughout his ministry (Acts 28:23, 30–31), positively identified the location of the kingdom of God in Romans 14:17, and clearly proclaimed that he had received his ministry through a revelation from the Lord and not from men (Gal. 1:6–11; Acts 20:24–25). And one of the magnificent seven listed in Acts 6:5b named Philip (the evangelist)(Acts 21:8) also preached the kingdom message (Acts 8:12).

Paul wrote to the church at Galatians AD 53–55 and was already aware and concerned that a failure to preach the one true gospel was already occurring (Gal. 1:6–7). Realizing that the gospel of the kingdom was Jesus's initial, consistent, and post-resurrection message, then ask yourself whether your denomination provides even one class on the message of the kingdom in its Bible school, college, or seminary. selah

So which gospel are you now preaching, teaching, declaring, and, most importantly, walking out (your lifestyle)? I have a very strong sense that we will be held accountable for failure to clearly proclaim this pivotal message (Matt. 4:17, 23, 6:33, 9:35, 24:14; Mark 1:15; Luke 4:43). This is the one message in the Bible that satan seems to have the greatest concern about. Jesus declares this fact in the parable of the sower in Matthew 13:11–19, Mark 4:10–15, and Luke 8:1–12. Please notice that this is recorded in all three of the Synoptics and that Jesus identifies satan himself, not one of his minions, as the one that comes to steal this vital message.

We simply must remember that satan was in heaven and is fully aware of the importance of this message. It seems profoundly clear that the message of the kingdom must not be underestimated. Let us again revisit Jesus's words in Matthew 24:14, "And this gospel of the kingdom will be preached in all the world as a witness to all the nations, and then the end will come."

Could the import of this message be expressed more succinctly? I fail to see how.

# Chapter 8—Transition Beyond Wildest Imagination

Since my earliest years, I have been a witness on many occasions when the healing power and miracle-working presence of God was manifested. In fact, I have personally been the recipient of such favor on many occasions. In those early years, however, my sense is that the display of the power of the Holy Spirit came about as a result of the agreement of other believers with mature faith rather than as a result of my personal faith quotient. What I want to request is that your consideration be given to this observation by contrasting the words of Jesus to His disciples, "O you of little faith" (Matt. 14:31, 16:8) with His words regarding the Centurion, "Assuredly, I say to you, I have not found such great faith, not even in Israel!" (Matt. 8:10).

It's also most interesting to note the fact that all three Synoptic Gospels record that Jesus put out the unbelieving skeptics in the raising of Jairus's daughter (Matt. 9:25; Mark 5:40; Luke 8:54). It seems quite clear that faithlessness (unbelief) was not tolerated in this instance.

My purpose for addressing this is to consider that, since the Lord has confirmed that there are in fact different levels of faith, we should recognize the necessity and advantages of remaining in the Word since faith comes by hearing the Word of God (Rom. 10:17). And please note that, for me, hearing is not to be confused with listening. Perhaps you too have listened to many Bible verses and various songs countless times throughout your life, yet are unable to accurately recall even one complete verse of scripture or song. Hearing is needed for us to grow our faith; thus in order to hear, someone needs to be speaking, and we need to be hearing (receiving in our spirit) the words that are spoken.

So whenever possible, please consider reading God's Word aloud if you are not already doing so. Are you in agreement with the statement that there is power in the spoken Word or, even more important, the Lord's declaration in John 6:63b, "The words that I speak to you are spirit, and they are life." There is such a powerful component added when you hear those words of God exiting your lips (and, of course, the lips of others) and entering your hearing portals.You will be profoundly and pleasantly surprised at the increased effectiveness of your Bible reading/devotion/quiet/soaking and memorization when you adopt this procedure.

Every bit as important is to develop an ongoing intimate fellowship with Him to grow our faith from little to great if we are to have any hope of arriving at the level spoken of by Jesus when He stated that the works He did we would do and greater than those. Additionally we know that, because of a lack of faith, Jesus did no mighty works in His own hometown (Mark 6:1–5), which substantiates that the existence of little faith or lack of faith is certain to hinder the quality and quantity of work that God desires to perform. The purpose for addressing this is to encourage every sincere believer to determine to mature to a level at which we fully expect that great signs, wonders, and miracles will occur every time two or more faith-mature Christ followers come into agreement (Matthew 18:19).

Am I at the ultimate level that I personally desire to be? Absolutely not, but I am well beyond where I began. I have reached the point where much more frequently than ever before I sense the Holy Spirit rest upon me and find my inner spirit rising in defiance to conditions threatened or caused by the evil one or any such malevolent events agreed to by someone who is ignorant of God's promise to change those circumstances that seem otherwise impossible, even to a majority of eyewitnesses.

Frequently emanating from deep inside and subsequently coming off my lips, I hear words such as, "No, we (kingdom kids) are not having that," and an unusual elevation of expectation surges to the forefront with the certainty that the effectual, fervent prayer of a person in right standing with the kingdom of God can achieve much.

Rest assured that this sort of declaration is not to be hurled directly into the face of a physician nor that of any unbeliever; thus in some circumstances, the refusal to accept an unacceptable prognosis is to be initially rejected internally or perhaps openly at a later time and in the presence of agreeing believers.

The respectful question posed to a physician when he proclaims an expected negative result can be, "Doctor, are you saying it will take a miracle to reverse this condition?"

The obvious advantage to this approach is that the one that reverses the predicted negative outcome is the very one that receives the glory, honor, and praise. And what could possibly be better than that? Additionally we must ever remember that, the greater the size of the mountain before us, the more it brings with it the certainty of an even greater gift that the Father wants to give us, "And my God shall supply ALL your need according to His riches in glory by Christ Jesus" (Phil. 4:19). It is an extravagant truth in which to rejoice and, as well, to rest.

Three occurrences of such righteous rising up that quickly come to mind all relate to newborns. The first was a child born with a body weight of one pound and one ounce. You read that correctly. 1 pound, 1 ounce. This birth was announced in February 2007 at a Sunday morning adult Bible class. We were then told that the pediatrician declared that the baby would not live, but if by some extremely unlikely chance he should survive, the family should fully expect him to have severe handicaps and disabilities for the balance of his life.

Well, for me to tell you that righteous indignation permeated our hearts and souls would be the understatement of the decade. As for myself, I recall thinking that our mortal enemy satan (the murderer)(John 8:44) has targeted children since Cain and Abel and can be expected to continue to attack these innocents until time ceases to exist. Need I mention abortion?

The Holy Spirit rose up in us, and we all agreed that we would not receive this negative report. We began to intercede on the baby's behalf, both believing and fully expecting a complete reversal of the prognosis. It became readily apparent that the Lord was fully engaged in this as "little" Vincent (and I call him "inVincible") began to show very consistent and obvious improvement. He has now celebrated his tenth birthdate, performed his piano recital, and is totally normal in every respect. Yes, the Lord has yet again turned to good what the enemy had meant for evil.

The second occurrence was in August 2009 when we were summoned to the intensive care unit of Santa Rosa Children's Hospital in San Antonio. The parents informed us that, due to a birth defect, the newborn baby had a hole in his heart and, as a result, would need an operation in which a heart-regulating device would necessarily be implanted.

Immediately upon receipt of this information, my spirit rose up. The bold and power-filled presence of the Holy Spirit overshadowed me, and as before, the words "No, we're not receiving this" resounded within my spirit and then erupted from my lips as throne room prayer (We have been seated with Him in heavenly places. (Eph. 2:6).

Spirit-enabled profound proclamation flowed from my lips. As the child lay cuddled in my palms, I looked into the face of this innocent, and with heaven-inspired compassion, trembling voice, and many human tears, words like these came forth,

> Lord, your Word tells us that little children represent the kind of humility and simple faith required to enter the kingdom of heaven (Luke 18:16–17), and your enemy is yet again attempting to thwart your plan for kingdom growth by his savage and treacherous means. We declare complete and total healing upon this child, healing which you already made provision for at Calvary some two thousand years ago (1 Peter 2:24).

Friends, there is passive praying, and then there is passionate praying. Throne room prayer is so obviously heaven-initiated and anointed that absolutely no human confirmation is needed. As a matter of fact, any believer or sincere seeker who is in the presence of such prayer can quickly know without any person telling him or her that this kind of prayer is heaven-inspired. It seems to be a combination of righteous indignation directed specifically at satan and simultaneously undergirded by the God kind of faith, not unlike a huge locomotive that clearly can not be stopped.

And just listen to the result of such prayer. The operation was scheduled for the same day as the above prayer, and fifteen minutes before the operation was to begin, a review was made and it was determined to be no longer necessary, and the operation was cancelled. What further proof do you require to know whether Abba Father wishes to answer your prayer?

Oh, by the way, this miracle boy is all the boy that a boy can be and has now celebrated his seventh birthdate without any mechanical device. Any doubt as to whom the glory, honor, and praise should be directed?

The third event occurred in November 2014 and demonstrates the same pattern of attack as before. Ethan Allan was a newborn, and his heart was racing dangerously at 320 beats per minute. Medication was administered. He was in the children's intensive care unit, and the doctors were advising that he would require ongoing medication and treatment for an undetermined, but extended period of time.

You should know that a rising up of faith occurred as mentioned before, as prayer was sent heavenward in the ICU unit on behalf of this innocent. You will be pleased to know that little Ethan is where he should be, at home in the loving arms of family amidst a celebration of the Great Physician that enabled such healing (1 Peter 2:24).

Let me assure you of a very important series of facts. I am not a superstar. I am not perfect. There still remains an occasional day when beneath an Elijah juniper (broom) tree (1 Kings 19:4) is where you may find me. But there are, all honor accrue to the Lord, many more days when I choose (and notice that it is my choice) to believe that I am who He says I am, determined to do what He says I can do, step out in boldness (Holy Spirit upon me), and choose to direct a frontal assault on the kingdom of darkness.

Look, if our Leader says that all authority (Matt. 28:18) (*exousia*, Greek) has been given to Him in heaven and earth (which means that someone else has no authority and care to guess who), unless I agree with him (satan) in opposition to what God says. Jesus further tells me that all that He has done can be done by me and then recalling the parable of the nobleman and the minas (Luke 19:11–13), its kingdom of God implication, and His admonition for each of us to do business (Luke 19:13) until He returns, it seems clear enough to me that we are to be totally engaged in conducting the Master's business with a full measure of expectation, hope, faith, and bold declaration (2 Cor. 4:13) combined with the certainty that no external entity can deter us from our spiritually appointed tasks!

Are you up for this opportunity? This kind of ongoing ministry is not reserved solely for great faith healers or pastors. Nor is it just for graduates of Bible schools or seminaries. No indeed. Read Matthew 10:8, 11:11 and Luke 7:28, and you will quickly observe that such results are in fact extended to, and expected of, every resident of the kingdom of God.

Let's just visit Matthew 10:7–8 and see whether we are following Jesus's commission in its entirety. Notice that Jesus's words are, "And as you go, preach, saying, 'The kingdom of heaven is at hand. Heal the sick, cleanse the lepers, raise the dead, cast out demons. Freely you have received, freely give.'"

Did you notice that Jesus said to heal the sick, cleanse the lepers, raise the dead, and cast out demons? He did not say to pray that the sick would be healed. Nor did He say to pray that the lepers would be cleansed. Nor did He say to pray that the dead would be raised. And He also did not say to pray that demons would be cast out.

No, He told His disciples to perform those activities, and He would never command anything of His disciples that they were not able to perform. That would be unjust. Now please recall with me that Jesus performed all those activities and that He further stated that the works He did we would do and greater than these because He would go to the Father. And all this was performed before the day of Pentecost. The *dunamis* power of the Holy Spirit was yet to be given.

This fact makes it obvious to me that even greater results were to be expected after the arrival of the Holy Spirit (Acts 1:8). And remember that Jesus declared that he who is least in the kingdom of God was greater than John the Baptist. And the apostle Paul clearly specified the location of the kingdom of God as being in the Holy Spirit (Rom. 14:17). There is such a harvest remaining to be finished. It is so clear that we must finish the Master's stated business.

So how about divine appointments? Do such things really occur? Bear with me as two are presented ultimately for your consideration and decision. My wife Cindy and I took off four days in September 2012 to celebrate our twelfth wedding anniversary. It was a wonderful celebration, especially when you consider the two wonder-filled Jehovah Sneaky events that occurred.

On Saturday morning, Cindy shared a somewhat curious dream she had during the night. She explained that, in her dream, she had seen a lady with medium brown hair with bangs. She couldn't determine the length of hair. It might have been tied in back. She said she didn't know the lady. She was attractive with a distinctive face. We agreed to agree and asked the Lord to reveal the significance in His timing.

Later that same morning, we decided to go to lunch in the city of New Braunfels to revisit the restaurant where I had proposed to her some twelve-plus years prior. As we were walking toward the restaurant, Cindy asked me to walk a bit slower, and while the reason was unclear at the time, it would shortly become obvious to me.

Our waiter was named Gilbert, a quite pleasant gentleman and very attentive. I was drawn to watch him as he dutifully went about his assignments, which is very unlike me. As I watched him, I could not help but notice an observable limp in his walk.

I commented to Cindy about this and then felt led to get one of the "Trust me. I have everything under control--Jesus", business cards out of my wallet for presentation to Gilbert.

I had determined to ask him for permission to pray for his limp, but in any event, I intended to give the card to him. I introduce it alternately as my "boss's" or "elder brother's" business card and use it for witnessing. At the bottom of the card is Jeremiah 33:3. I tell the recipient that this is the contact number and that you never get a busy signal and He will always answer, you are never placed on hold and there is never a long-distance charge. And I turn it upside down and ask the person to read it. I then watch for his or her facial reaction as he or she reads it (It's such a joy to see their reaction). You might want to know that I have them professionally printed on cream-colored stock and carry a supply with me for impromptu witnessing...they are a wonderful conversation starter!

I told Cindy what was planned, and when he returned, I commented on his limp and told him that, when Jesus was on earth, he healed countless persons and that He was the same yesterday, today, and forever (Heb. 13:8). I asked if he were aware of that, to which he replied that he was. He added that he had damaged his Achilles tendon some eight months prior and that it was slow in healing. After receiving his permission, we prayed softly with him with our eyes open and could visibly see that he was impacted by the presence of the Holy Spirit. We gave the card to him and shared the veracity of the words on the card. He thanked us, put the card in his pocket, and returned to his activity.

After he left, Cindy looked at me with an expression of excitement and informed me that, as we exited our vehicle in arriving at the restaurant, she had felt a pain in her Achilles. We were both amazed and thrilled as we have come to understand that God loves people enough to reveal facts to his servants (Amos 3:7) before events come to pass.

Oh, we understand that He doesn't cause the pain. Rather He allows it, remembering Job's troubles, so we may pray for His restorative healing power to be manifested as needed. We also fully recognize that, in those cases where we have injured or exerted ourselves, those are not the same circumstances as in this case, for Cindy had neither overexercised nor injured her achilles, in short, it wasn't her pain. God chose this method to give us advance notice and the subsequent confirmation. These types of events are so wondrous when you consider the extent to which God will go to outwardly demonstrate His unfathomable love. So on Monday, September 10, we elected to go to Austin, Texas, to one of our very favorite homestyle cooking restaurants. We were shortly escorted to our booth, and our waitress appeared soon after to take our drink and menu order. As she went to the computer to place our order, I took notice of her shoes, again very unusual for me, and then described them to Cindy (she was behind Cindy). She told me they were ballerina shoes, they were in style, and that they were a quite comfortable work shoe. Again as with Gilbert the day prior, I was drawn to observe her demeanor.

While she was quite professional, I had the sense she was masking some event(s) in her life, and I then commented to Cindy concerning this discernment and asked if she would be comfortable with my discussing it with Tiffany. Cindy agreed. It's always an excellent idea to let your prayer partner know the plan so he or she can be in agreement (Matthew 18:19).

As with Gilbert, I felt led to get a "Trust me" card from my wallet. When Tiffany returned, and I felt led (God's timing is so very important.), I commented that she was very professional but appeared to be masking some difficulty in her life.

I continued with, "God wants you to know that He loves you and He knows the number of hair on your head (Luke 12:7). And He keeps your tears in His bottle" (Psalm 56:8).

As I shared with eyes open, it was quite obvious that she was very powerfully impacted. She swallowed, actually more like a gulp, when impacted by the presence of the Holy Spirit. At that moment, for the very first time, Cindy looked directly at Tiffany. We finished the talk, prayed for her, and gave her the "Trust me" card. She choked out the words "thank you," put the card in her apron, and, visibly touched, daubed her eyes as she hurriedly went back to the rear of the restaurant and out of sight. Now prepare yourself for the big shock. Cindy then told me, "Mike, that is the face of the person I saw in my dream (Friday night/Saturday morning)."

We were so indescribably overwhelmed at the lengths to which God will go to demonstrate His inestimable love for one individual. Just think about this. God would give Cindy a dream two days prior. We would be led to choose to drive the fifty-plus miles from Seguin to Austin to a restaurant where He knew one individual named Tiffany would be working and she would be assigned to our booth. Then God would so powerfully impact my sensitivity to His plan and would enable us to be able to minister to her immediate and deepest need. How could anyone question or even wonder whether such a compassionate Father loves every individual on this planet?

Without a doubt, these two events alone clearly demonstrate that He truly will leave ninety-nine and pursue one lost sheep. And when we recall that He is no respecter of person (Acts 10:34) and further that there are clearly no coincidences in the life of a believer, we should consider every human contact of every day as a potential opportunity for each of us to be a servant-minister to address the needs of yet another of God's creation. And we need not be a superstar, rather a willing servant sensitive to every need of those that God places in our path.

These two events are a variation on a teaching I had received several years earlier from my then-pastor/mentor, Donald K. Wiehe. He stated that he had recently learned of an effective witnessing method to be used with waitstaff is to declare that you will soon be praying over your food and wonder if there is/are events in his or her life or the life of a family member, coworker, or neighbor for which he or she would desire prayer to be made. It is helpful to suggest that the need for prayer could be for such areas as employment, an injury, illness, or despair. This helps to "jumpstart" their thought process.

I have used this approach countless times and have never had even one occasion where a person told me that he or she didn't want prayer. There have been several occurrences where the person returned minutes later and declared that he or she had just recalled the plight of a loved one, friend, or coworker and stated that he or she would appreciate prayer for this person.

I had first used this method at a Taco Cabana Tex-Mex Restaurant on an earlier occasion. I prayed for the injured uncle of a cashier who had suffered a hip-damaging fall from a tall ladder, and upon returning slightly more than a week later, that same cashier excitedly told me that a physician told her uncle that it was a miracle how quickly and completely his leg/hip had been restored.

Please consider adding this technique to your servant arsenal. I have received so very many opportunities to witness to and pray for waitpersons, and I am confident you will as well. Please know that you are demonstrating compassion (means to suffer with; an internal affection; tender mercy) and you are sending a powerful message that you care about them. And also know that it doesn't go unnoticed by them. The aftermath of joy is certain to quickly follow each of these faithful servant events. I am personally convinced that this great joy is what Jesus referred to when the disciples urged Him to eat. His reply in John 4:31-34 is such a classic response,"I have food to eat of which you do not know". Doing the will of the Father brings such joy and thus is so wonderfully satisfying. Try it, you'll like it! Guaranteed!

I lost a family member in 2010, and in the process, a series of events occurred that will further support the lengths to which heaven will go to assure the opportunity for every person to access eternal life. My daughter called me at work to let me know that my brother-in-law was in intensive care and not expected to survive. She gave me the name of the hospital. I notified the property manager was granted permission to depart, left soon after and proceeded to where I understood him to be.

At the hospital reception desk, I gave his name, received his room number, and proceeded to the room. Arriving at the room, I saw that tubes were in his mouth/nose, and after calling his name and receiving no response, I decided to sit, read my Bible, and pray for his recovery so I could, at the least, ascertain his eternal relationship with the Lord.

Some thirty minutes elapsed, and an adult female arrived and approached the patient. After a few moments, I asked if she were a friend of the family, and she stated that this was her husband. I realized that an error had been made. Both men had the same name and very similar physical appearance. Do you think it possible that God wanted prayer to be spoken over this man's life as well? I have no doubt! After all, He's not willing that any perish (2 Peter 3:9).

I quickly called my daughter and learned that the correct hospital was on the southeast side of the city and not southwest, as was previously understood. I began to pray as I drove the thirty or so minutes to the correct hospital, asking the Lord to keep Bob both alive and conscious until my arrival so I could pray with him.

Upon arrival, it was apparent that several family members had gathered with several waiting their opportunity to go into his small cubicle, one or two at a time. I prayed while waiting my turn, again asking that Bob would be both alive and conscious and able to respond to questions about the state of his relationship with the Lord.

After perhaps ten minutes, his eldest daughter, upon seeing me, motioned for me to enter. Then observing that Bob's mouth and nose had tubes inserted, I called his name and recognized that it was difficult for him to speak and impossible to understand his responses. I told him that I would take his hand and he could respond by squeezing my hand once for a yes or twice for a no.

He agreed and acknowledged by squeezing once. I reminded him that we had been down lots of roads together and we both had done some things with which we were pleased and other things that we knew were wrong, in fact, were obviously sin. One squeeze. I asked him if he believed that Jesus could forgive his sin. One squeeze. And then I asked him that, if he were able to speak, would he ask Jesus for His total forgiveness. One more very firm squeeze followed by a strong guttural expression, which was most certainly a response in the affirmative. Then thanking the Lord for His extravagant mercy, we shortly ended the prayer.

A few hours later, Bob expired. You may be thinking that is a great ending, and certainly that was the desired result. But God often chooses to go one step beyond our expectation.

Exactly three days later, I arose at 5:25 am to go prepare for the day at hand, and as I entered the bathroom, I sensed a strong presence. And from inside my being, I heard Bob's voice as clearly as I had heard it aloud thousands of times before simply say, "Thanks, Mike."

Folks, rest assured that I recognize Bob's voice when I hear it. I don't pretend to know how the Father does this kind of thing, and frankly I don't care how He does it. He is certainly omnipotent, immeasurably loving, and He is completely trustworthy. Thus, He can do whatever He decides. It's simply further proof that He cares so much that He can choose to unexpectedly use even the supernatural to further demonstrate the vastness of His indescribable love. And anyway, what we term supernatural is natural to him. Yes, indeed!

In the spring of 2013, a group of men from the church elected to attend the annual men's retreat in the beautiful Texas Hill Country near Kerrville. Our district men's leader selected a young pastor to open the weekend with prayer. As mentioned previously, there is prayer, and then there is throne room prayer. He accepted the microphone and then deliberately paused reverently for perhaps seven or eight seconds, which, in retrospect, I perceived was to obtain direction from the Holy Spirit.

And from the first sentence of his declaration, it was overwhelmingly apparent that this gentleman had not simply talked about prayer, just taught on prayer, or just read books on prayer. Neither had he only listened to others pray; nor was his prayer simply a product of attending prayer seminars. It most certainly was not memorized prayer. No, it was immediately and inarguably apparent that he had in time past made a conscious decision to put in place, to schedule, and to commit to an ongoing, intimate dialogue with heaven and that, like Daniel of old, this was his custom since early days (Dan. 6:10).

I was so powerfully impacted that I could hardly wait to express my utter delight and total appreciation for this most extravagant communication within my hearing. Folks, I have heard thousands of prayers in my life. Many were very excellent, but there exists a level of prayer that is so glorious that it can only be described as heaven-originated, and indeed this was just such a one.

As soon as possible, I made my way to this anointed man, introduced myself to him, and told him how profoundly impacting that his prayer had been. As you may have already guessed, he told me that both he and his wife each had intensive prayer ministry both in their church for the men and women of the church and the people of the city. And that was just the beginning. He then asked if I would permit him to pray with me.

After my delighted response of absolutely yes, he began to declare/impart the following events that I would experience or participate in. He stated that I would be involved in children's ministry; children and adults that I prayed for would be healed (which I discerned to mean both physical and spiritual healing); I would actively participate in world missions; I would be a teacher of the word; I would author a book and other similar declarations.

My mouth practically dropped open. Understand that we had never met before or talked; nor did we have any mutual acquaintances or friends. (My pastor had not previously met him.) But get this. I am in the fifteenth year of children's ministry. You have read of the miraculous healing of three wonderful children in this tome. There have been mission trips to Jamaica (2012–2013), Kenya (2011), and Mexico (1999 and 2001). I have taught the Word of God in a Friday night care group with the previously mentioned Mike and Rachel since April 2010, and you are reading the first book authored by my hand, but, of course, guided by the Holy Spirit.

This kind of accuracy can only come forth via the Holy Spirit through persons who are consistently in contact with the heavenly realm. Perhaps you would like to know that the first and middle names of this pastor were John Paul. Significant? And, oh yes, his surname also has a kingdom relevance (think cross). Draw your own conclusion, but at the least, I think you can agree that they are certainly significant biblical names.

In 2009, the urge to begin to chronicle events and the charge of Habakkuk 2:2, "write the vision and make it plain on tablets, that he may run who reads it" impacted me, and the title of "A Journal of One Seeker's Adventures with the Holy Spirit" seemed to be an appropriate moniker. Thus the prologue of this manuscript came directly from the first two pages of that yellow spiral notebook.

The first adventure recorded occurred early on the morning of August 22, 2009. Cindy and I had been following the Advanced Prophetic Equipping Conferences televised on God TV with the desired end result to be an ability to move in power, revelation, and supernatural prophetic ministering on an ongoing and consistent basis and without interruption. This is obviously achievable only by both having been born again and experiencing an insatiable hunger and thirst for the deepest intimacy with the Lord through the direction of the Holy Spirit.

We had been stirred deeply within and were determined to savor the deep things and other attainable spiritual riches of God. This bold determination was pivotal in the following event that occurred sometime before I awakened at 0452 hours. Let me preface this with the fact that I had not been a frequent dreamer previously and can't recall having dreamed in color prior to this event.

In my dream, which included the appearance of an approaching darkness, I was driving a vehicle along an unpaved and curvy road when I arrived at a circular stockade-type structure in the center of the road. The posts comprising the structure were of three varying heights.The outermost circle of posts was the shortest at about three feet in height. The middle ones were about five feet tall. And the innermost circle was comprised of posts that were at least seven feet in height. I was unable to see what, if anything, was housed inside of them.

There was, however, a genuine concern as to how I could get into the inside of the structure and access its contents, which I very clearly understood encompassed a treasure of great value. I had parked my vehicle to the left of the circular stockade and exited it only to be immediately approached by what I would describe as a native witch doctor with his upper-center front teeth missing, clutching a staff in his right hand and, in his left, swinging a small blue bag in my direction.

Initially I felt the bag might strike me, but it did not, and he placed it behind me. Immediately following, two teenagers (one boy and one girl) approached me with what I felt were useless items. The boy offered drinking straws; the girl offered some napkins. I felt that they wanted me to buy these items. They were attired in what reminded me of Holland-style dress: sharp points on the collars, blue-colored vests, and maize-colored shirts and blouses beneath the vests. I next observed that the road was bordered by barbed wire fencing and then saw a lioness and two birds of prey (like buzzards) that gave me the feeling they were lurking about with a desire to devour.

The dream ended. I awakened and decided to check the time and observed it was 0452 hours. I felt the time was significant and made a mental note of it, and based upon a teaching given by the Reverend Bill Johnson (Bethel Church in Redding, California), I felt it to be a scriptural reference. I wanted to understand the implications of the dream and asked Cindy if she had any revelation as to its meaning, as she had on more than a few previous occasions demonstrated an obvious understanding of dreams.

She said she felt led to tell me that the Lord Himself wanted to deliver the meaning of this dream to me. And sensing she was correct, we then proceeded on our early morning walk with pet Rudy in tow. As we walked, I sought the Lord for understanding, and following are my spirit-led impressions of that dream:

1. I turned aside to see what God was doing (Ex. 3:3–4).
2. People will offer useless items (even sell them) into our spiritual lives.
3. Outside the kingdom, there are dogs and sorcerers (Rev. 22:15).
4. God has riches that are to be searched out (the stockade), and the enemy will constantly distract, attempt to intimidate, deter, or desire to hide them from us (Prov. 25:2; Neh. 4).

So then, after returning from our walk, I felt led to take my awakening time (0452) and look for confirming scripture. My Bible was on the serving counter in the kitchen and was open to Isaiah 43. Perceiving that to be significant, I was drawn to go to Isaiah 45:2. Recall the time of awakening was 0452 hours, and that is noteworthy because the book of Isaiah had passed through my mind as I sought the Lord about the dream during our morning walk.

I was so wonderfully amazed and overcome as my eyes fell on the verse of Isaiah 45:2,

> "I will go before you and make the crooked places straight; I will break in pieces the gates of bronze and cut the bars of iron. I will give you the treasures of darkness and hidden riches of secret places, that you may know that I, the Lord, who call you by your name, am the God of Israel."

Words cannot express the sense of God's desire to make Himself profoundly obvious to me. Lord, what is man? In this case, I, Mike, and mindful. Your mind is full of Him? While I am certain that I shall not soon forget this wonderful event, I felt encouraged, even confident, that this kind of display would be repeated unendingly and perhaps even more frequently as long as I consistently seek his face (Ps. 27:8) and make additional conscious decisions to intentionally promote intimate fellowship with him (Phil. 3:10; Rev. 3:20).

God is such a lover that He has promised to me from His Word that if I will draw nigh unto Him He will draw nigh unto me (James 4:8). "My soul (my mind, will, and emotions),wait silently for God alone, for my expectation is from Him" (Ps. 62:5). That phrase to "wait silently for God alone" immediately creates for me a mental picture of an ultra-professional waiter in a five-star restaurant with a cloth neatly draped over his arm and his tray perched upon his fingertips. He is 100 percent attentive to every request made of him and fully determined to fulfill every one of those requests without delay.

And then it hit me. That is an exact depiction of how the relationship is to be between me (the waiter/servant) and the

Great King (the one to be served). Can you receive it? I choose to become one of those who are determined to perform it.

God uses many different ways to demonstrate His concern for us and to fully disclose the vastness of His love. One such display occurred during my assignment as a doorkeeper (Ps. 84:10b) on a Sunday evening. The primary part of that activity was to greet and direct arriving worshipers to areas in the sanctuary where seating was available.

On this evening, I was drawn to observe where a particular congregant chose to sit. The pastor was leading choruses, and this voice inside me was prompting me to share a specific scripture of encouragement with this person. Well, I was quite reticent about following this leading to the extent that internally I heard myself saying, "But Lord, I've never even seen this person before, and it might be thought presumptuous of me to take such an action."

At this point, the chorus seemed to be coming to an end, and I felt sure that I would have used that as an excuse to avoid the assignment, but the pastor signaled to the musicians to continue. And again the urging returned with such an intensity that I was now resisting the leading by leaning back against the wall of the sanctuary and again internally saying, "But Lord, this person is a lady, and she may think I am out of line by such action."

By this time, the insistence was such that it felt as if a hand was in my back pushing me forward, so finally I moved to a position one row behind, leaned over the pew, and apologetically began, "Ma'am, I have never done this before, but I feel strongly led to share Jeremiah 33:3 with you." I reached the point of "Call unto me and I will answer thee," and a fountain of tears and the accompanying emotion burst forth like a dam erupting as she blurted out, "You will never know how much this means to me."

I have to tell you that it was very obvious that God was filling a great need in her life, but what subsequently became equally obvious was that God was teaching me to hear His voice and to be obedient to His assignment (think trust and obey). I clearly know that to be the case because, the very next Sunday eve, He gave me a different verse to deliver to a different worshiper with a similar result, but you can rest assured that He did not have to tell me three times. No indeed, once was quite sufficient.

"Don't fight your fear. Feed your faith!" That's exactly what he said, and I have chosen not to forget the impact of that statement. The speaker was David Coote, laudable president of International Bible College (I.B.C.) in San Antonio, and he was a guest speaker at Trinity Church at the invitation of Pastor Allen Randolph. It would be more than twenty-five years later before I would fully grasp the significance of those seven words. Oh, it was apparent to me at that time that the measure of my faith was most significant and the ability to continue to walk in a level of great faith was assured by my consistency in hearing the Word of God (Rom. 10:17).

What I was to consider many years later was that the planet on which we live is a problem-solving environment. Because we live in a fallen world, we have come to be exposed to a worldly thinking protocol that has us often traveling a path of fear and uncertainties. But the approach that Dr. Coote was advocating was driven by a heaven-borne perspective. Since there is no pain, sorrow, disappointment, or other negatives, including fear in heavenly places, there is no need to approach any of the negative offerings of this fallen world with anything other than a heaven-demonstrated positive approach. Do you see it? God does not choose to concentrate on negatives or darkness. He drives it out with heaven-created light. "Let there be light, and there was light!" It is so obvious that I need not reinvent the wheel; rather I must simply follow the example demonstrated by the Lord. And further, since Jesus resides inside me and my circumstances are between my ears, He is in the midst of those circumstances. Hence, there is clearly no reason to allow fear.

During the same time period, heaven chose to exhibit yet another example of memories that never lose their luster. A wonderful expositor of the Word and a Scot with a quite delightful brogue, the Reverend Campbell McAlpine gifted Trinity Church with four days of unforgettable teaching and exhortation that impacted me so wonderfully that I recorded the dates of July 7-10, 1985, and I then highlighted the specific scripture. I have continued to commemorate this event by transferring forward the profoundness of that event to successive Bibles. Please know that the fragrance and presence of the Holy Spirit continues to hover over the memory of those four pivotal days.

Every time I read Isaiah 66:1-2 as well any time those scripture are recited, an instant drawing pulls me to the reverence and overarching of that first moment. Indeed, the delivery of the Word by God's servant was wonderfully anointed, but do not miss the greater point that, when heaven invades any event, the significance of that visit is not soon past and, in many instances, is never pushed to the rear of human memory. Physicians tell us that events or activity in our brain leaves creases upon our brain, and since God is an heart-oriented father, I am personally convinced that He can place indelible heart marks. Perhaps these marks could be thought of as memory tattoos or "tats"? Though not visible externally, they are nevertheless permanently etched on the heart and could be said to become the most highly prized in every collection.Each time any passionate seeker/worshiper directs his or her soul to follow hard after Him, he or she makes a considered determination to capture the indescribable significance of that moment. Oh, the impact that occurs within when I hear or recite those words, "But on this one will I look: on him who is poor and of a contrite spirit, and who trembles at my word."

Just think of the implication of those words. God looks to certain people. We know that fact, but how intensely and how frequently do we let it impact the innermost depths of our being? King David adds additional support to this certain people declaration with "My eyes shall be on the faithful of the land" (Ps. 101:6).

Folks, ponder the fact that the Hubble Telescope has enabled the discovery of billions of galaxies, each with billions of stars that are now known to exist. And then couple that with the knowledge that the God of all creation counts the number of those stars and further calls them all by name (Ps.147:4). It simply overloads my understanding. (Hey, let me just assure you that I have 2nd & 3rd cousins in California whose names I do not know.) And now I am drawn to contemplate the assurance that this unfathomable and humanly undefinable entity looks to certain people? And further when I recall that this awesome entity chooses to inscribe my name upon the palms of His hands (Isa. 49:15-16), I am unable to contain the accompanying, totally overwhelming joy. Just try to imagine the size of palms that contain the engraved names of every person that has ever accepted the extravagant gift of His beloved son...I am speechless.

Simply stated, His ways are truly past finding out. My, my, my, what a King, what a God, what a Creator, what a Lover. And since I am incapable of praising Him sufficiently in my one relatively short lifetime, I determinedly choose to praise Him throughout life everlasting.

Yet another demonstration of the diversity of the Father's good and perfect gifts found its way to a plot of land that we had been led to consider as a potential site for our future retirement. Actually, as Bishop Vincent Theophilus Williams, appropriately named "The Billy Graham of Jamaica," so very powerfully reminded me. "Kingdom kids don't ever retire they just re-fire."

A valued friend from church had located the land, seriously considered buying it, and then subsequently decided upon an alternate location. Aware that we had actively been searching for an extended period of time, he reminded me of the land and suggested we might want to view it.

Cindy and I previously had agreed that we would not select or even consider any property until we had an "aha" moment including a certainty in each of our spirits that this was "the" place. Some prerequisites that both of us preferred included some elbow room, sufficient space for a garden, definitely out in the country, away from bothersome traffic and its accompanying noise, yet not too distant from church, shopping, and medical facilities. And we especially desired a plot on a hill with views in at least two directions (for the wraparound porch we had envisioned) and more than one exit path in the event of flood conditions. And just as important, we had sought and located an open floor plan that would accommodate and serve a Bible study (care group) as well as permit the hosting of visiting servants of the kingdom.

As you would expect, God heard the desires of both our hearts, and this was the place. We learned that a water well of 280-foot depth had already been drilled, and that the absolutely necessary submersible pump would be included and installed when the sale was consummated. As we discussed general information with those who would become our two closest neighbors, we learned (by tasting) that one neighbor had a very undesirable sulfur odor in their water. Another neighbor explained that, due to the hardness of the water and the very real likelihood of odor, we should most certainly plan on the installation of a water conditioning system. We weighed those recommendations, investigated our alternatives, had extended conversation (prayer) with our very best friends (Father, Son, and Holy Spirit), and made our choice. We chose to instead give the land and all its accoutrement to our Father and proceeded to declare that fact to Him. Further we were led to anoint every fence post on the 11.846 acres and, of course, the water well while we voiced our declaration, "Father, this is your property, and this is your water supply. Let it be exactly as you wish it to be." I don't mind telling you that we got some raised eyebrows when we shared this fact with some folk, including some "Christians"; nevertheless, we have reasonably soft and quite excellent tasting water in God's well. We fully anticipate that many of you will visit and "taste and see that the Lord (and His water) is good."

I heartily recommend this approach, and please don't deny it until you try it! One really exciting addendum to this event is that Cindy and I had been privileged to participate in a missions trip to Kenya in 2011, and the camp we stayed in while in the bush had been given the Masai warrior name of Namelok. We had agreed that, since we had similar terrain, we would refer to our ranch as Namelok and subsequently were thrilled to learn that the word Namelok translates into "sweet water." Coincidence? Not in our minds!

My purpose for sharing this sort of panorama of godly intervention is to make it quite clear that, just as the Father chooses a variety of methods to bring physical and spiritual healing to individuals, He uses that same unquantifiable wisdom (omniscience) to display His essence (God is love) in every aspect of every life of every person that has ever or will ever live. And not just for a lifetime, but rather for everlasting life!

I challenge you to locate a better contract (covenant) than that. Please rest assured no such contract exists. Our challenge is to be constantly aware of this fact and attuned to the presence of the Holy Spirit so that we never dismiss out of hand some very nearly undetectable urging within. Such an occurrence might prove to be a critical, perhaps even life-or-death matter as it evolves. We need continue to remember that it is a still, small voice for which we listen, and that requires that we be finely tuned and walk softly if we are to receive His summons. Further, we need to remember that we may be unable to hear His communique if we constantly have our ears flooded with the sounds of the plethora of electronic devices thrust upon us in our daily living. We must not forget to be still and know that He is God and that He is desirous of ongoing intimate contact. And as the logos, He is ever talking, but the burning question continues to be, "Am I consistently hearing?" Hmm, this calls for some intentional thought. Please excuse my necessary pause. selah

Recently while ruminating and dissecting the Lord's priestly prayer to the Father as recorded in John chapter 17, I was drawn to consider a phrase that curiously (to me, at least) continued to draw my attention to such an extent that I found it quite difficult to disregard. You most likely have observed it and very possibly have evaluated it, but please humor me as I work to develop it. In verse 2 we see the phrase,"to as many as you have given Him (Jesus)." Continuing in verse 6, there is the phrase "The men whom you have given me." Also in verse 9, it says, "Those whom you have given me." In verse 11, we see again,"Those whom you have given me." And finally in verse 12, there is, "Those whom you gave me."

What impacts me is that the Father chose these disciples as specific assignments for Jesus to teach, urge, exhort, rebuke, and build up, that is, to live a lifestyle before them that would ultimately afford them opportunity for entry into the kingdom and the skills necessary to replicate what had been demonstrated to them. My point is that Jesus was not expected to personally lead every individual person that He met into the kingdom. We know that, because in John 17:4 He declares that He "finished the work which you have given me to do." And we know as well that there were many who chose not to receive His message (John 6 :64, 66-67).

And the point of all this? Since the Father is no respecter of person, it seems certain that He has chosen certain specific people for both you and I, but the ones chosen for you are not necessarily in my area of responsibility and vice versa. Oh sure, you may water mine, and I may plant seed in yours, but ultimately, we both have different groups of accountability. So?

It seems that sometimes we have a tendency to feel downhearted if we aren't successful in leading every person we meet and especially, of course, all our family members into the safety of the heavenly portal. And the enemy just loves to use this as a tool of utter condemnation, especially when we are in a time of weakness or discouragement.

I am certainly not advocating that we halfheartedly serve any individual because we feel that he or she has not been assigned to us because it is quite conceivable that the person to whom he or she is assigned has not yet stepped up to the plate. And the Father may have chosen us to receive both the responsibility and reward for being instant season in and season out. I bring this personal discovery for your consideration to decide for yourself whether you believe that the Father may choose to show up and bring similar new insights to you when you decide to set aside unhurried time to delve into the richness of His Word with an insatiable desire and unbridled anticipation. You then are able to uncover the concealed delights of the Father as recorded in Proverbs 25:2, "It is the glory of God to conceal a matter, but the glory of kings (that is us, Rev.1:6) is to search out a matter." So, good hunting my fellow kings!

Now that we know that Jesus only did and said what He saw the Father doing and saying and since Jesus utilized various methods of healing, is it permissible to consider the possibility that the Father might appreciate a variety of prayer and worship methods as well? Our home church has two back-to-back Sunday morning services in which we worship in one and serve in the other.

And since there is no Sunday evening service, and after notifying our pastor, we chose to visit recently at a church in the capital city of Austin. We had heard that the Spirit of the Lord was powerfully evident in this house of worship and that there were some variations from what some might call the norm, but since we know that God has clearly notified us to behold that He will do a new thing (Isa. 43:19), we were not averse to this possibility.

As we entered the sanctuary, we noticed a reverent quietness with some perhaps thirty to forty persons scattered throughout. Upon the podium were six musicians, of which two were quietly praying as they gently stroked their instrument, while others were very softly tuning their instruments. And after a time, in muted voices, they began to communicate among themselves what Cindy and I supposed to be a direction to be taken.

After some ten or so minutes, the keyboard musician began to softly sing and was accompanied by the other musicians. The now fifty to sixty congregants were quietly moving about, exchanging hugs or handshakes or simply greeting each other. Some were sitting; a few were standing. Others were kneeling, but all were in an obvious reverent mode. Yet there was an observable, clearly detectable sense of expectation permeating the entire place.

Did you notice there was no corporate opening prayer and no formal declaration of a beginning? But let me be absolutely clear about this. There was clearly a strong presence. No one had to tell you, no declaration was needed, and no proclamation should have been made. And that certainty was apparent from the moment we entered the room. And friends, that was only the beginning. I immediately heard in my spirit, "Be still, and know that I am God" (Ps. 46:10). And rest assured, you could not help but know. For my part, it was powerfully obvious that this body of believers had arrived in a 100 percent fully expectant state of anticipation. There was no doubt in their mind that the manifest presence of the Holy One of Israel would be detectably evident throughout the evening.

This continued for one hour and ten glorious minutes, and then without any pomp or ceremony, the leader took the handheld microphone and began to share from memory some scripture, words of comfort, and declaration of the incomparable delight of dwelling in the presence and under the canopy of the kingdom of heaven. My sincere desire is that this type of hosting the presence can become a starting place for others to become willing to accept the certainty that some specific formula is not required. Rather the Father desires that we know that passion, invitation, expectation, agreement, and a sincere seeking for spiritual intimacy are all that is required to woo or draw Him (James 4:8) to occupy this earthly realm.

To accomplish this, we can join with as few as one other person since scripture has promised that, where two or three gather together in His name, He will be in the midst of them (Matt. 18:20). Please permit me to provoke you to become like the psalmist David in that your soul follows hard after the Lord's incomparable presence (Ps. 16:11). A very frequent and necessary reminder to the Father that we are truly appreciative of every good and perfect gift is certainly needed, but consider adding that you are not satisfied. You want more-much more-of His truly extravagant, indefinable, and awesome presence.

And God is not limited to just one method of creating such marvelous awareness of His existence and His desire to communicate both corporately and individually with His kids. Some events initiated by the Lord uniquely evoke such joy that you can find yourself just wanting to laugh aloud, perhaps chuckle, or yes, even giggle as you, in retrospect, revisit them. Perhaps it might best be described as joy at such an uncontainable level that, if an abnormal release is not employed, you feel you just might explode, much like an overfilled balloon.

Anyway, I don't recall exactly when it began, but it has surely been longer than four years ago, and it has grown in intensity and increased in frequency to such a level that it just must be shared. For me, it can start as early as 1:17, 3:00, 4:00, or 5:00 in the morning and is most prevalent on days when I have no early commitments scheduled and hence no alarm setting was needed. (And as a result, I am less likely to rush the event).

Then at heaven's predetermined time, my eyes open, and you need to know that, whenever my eyes open, my awareness is very quickly activated, that is, I am not slow to awaken. I shortly begin to receive input of thought and impression, and relevant scripture isn't far behind. On some occasions, the subject matter is pertinent to what I have pondered during recent daylight hours; however, almost as often there are refreshed ideas, those being some on which a significant amount of time has elapsed since last considered. And then there are also those that I feel were downloaded by heaven as I slumbered (Job 33:14-16).

Recently there was a leading to Psalm 63 in its entirety. That occurred when I was awakened at 0630 hours and was impressed to read in the book of Psalms as the words,

> Early will I seek you; my soul thirsts for you; my flesh longs for you in a dry and thirsty land ... thus I will bless you ... I will lift up my hands ... my mouth shall praise you with joyful lips ... when I remember you on my bed, I meditate on you in the night watches ... because you have been my help, therefore in the shadow of your wings I will rejoice.

It was then, right after "joyful" and "rejoice," coupled with "in the night watches," that I was reminded of Psalm 16:7 and continued reading to verse 11, and that brought a "rhema" moment as my eyes fell on, "You will show me the path of life; in your presence is fullness of joy; at your right hand are pleasures evermore."

This led to Acts 2:28 and "You have made known to me the ways of life; you will make me full of joy in your presence." And then it struck me that one of the day-to-day decisions that follows me throughout life is, "Which way should I go? Which path should I take?" And on the heels of all these followed Proverbs 3:6b, "And he shall direct your paths."

And then the brilliant million candlepower light came on-you know the one, the light that accompanies "rhema" words-as my eyes retraced the words: "IN YOUR PRESENCE is fulness of joy" and then you will make me full of joy IN YOUR PRESENCE." What's that you say, You will show me the path of life, and you have made known to me the ways of life. And this can all occur with fullness of joy if I am in your presence?

Wait just a minute here. I already know that an acceptable acrostic for JOY is Jesus Overarching You, and just how great is it to be bubbling over with unrestrained joy? Plus we already know that joy is not to be confused with happy. Happy lasts for a season, but heaven-dispensed joy is unaffected by emotion. So let me see if I've got this right. If I stay in your presence, I can expect fulness of joy. My, my, my, that is clearly a no-brainer.

Oh yes, you can absolutely count me among those intentionally determined to pursue your presence with total abandon, whether daytime, nighttime, or, of course, just anytime! And now, I'm bubbling over with unrestrained joy! Plus we already know my assignment becomes a concerted effort to achieve greater capacity so I am able to host a far greater quantity of His unfathomable and indefinable presence. Would you care to join me? I am continuously learning that He has an inexhaustible supply! What an encouragement that is, agree?

Well, you very likely recognize that there are those teaching/correcting times that are sure to follow. Most often, they aren't fun, but they are so needed. And some of those spiritual sessions are so sensitive that we would really rather they were never confronted. You know, just like when Paul withstood Peter "to the face" (Gal. 2:11-21) concerning his distinction of affiliation with Jews who had come to believe on Christ. Well, just walk down this path with me.

During my growing-up years, I frequently heard the original Americans referred to with insulting names, and there were also degrading names used to describe Hispanics. Similarly I heard African Americans viciously referred to. I heard Asian-Americans unkindly spoken of. And I heard Anglos referred to in a hurtful manner, all so insulting, demeaning, unkind, and certainly not a demonstration of loving one another.

Oh, how I wish I could tell you that I never heard such words come from the lips of those claiming to be followers of Jesus, but unfortunately that was not always the case either. But please, please, PLEASE stay with me until this is fully confronted. We must not be deceived into thinking that somehow or someday this sort of thing will just go away. Recall with me, please the definition of insanity: continuing to do what you have always done and expecting a different result.

And come on, renewed ones. We need each other. The task before us of "making disciples of all nations" is seemingly insurmountable unless/until we all become as one (John 17:20-23). And we had better know that this is a heart issue. We dare not think that we can get away with pretending to love one another outwardly, but remaining unregenerate internally because, as a man (humankind) thinks in his heart, that's who he is (Prov. 23:7).

So here comes the slam dunk. I'm reading in Acts 17, and upon reaching Acts 17:26, I am then abruptly stopped with the words, "And He (God) has made from one blood (Adam) every nation of men to dwell on all the face of the earth." And then I am compelled by the Holy Spirit to read those words again. And yes, twice more. And then it hits me. We are, like it or not, blood brethren. Oh, but that is not the end of the matter. No, sireee. Here is the tough part of this revelation to receive. When we degrade another person because of his or her skin color, physical characteristic, or some other externally detectable difference, we are choosing to ascribe less value to him or her. We had better know that we are not just insulting that person. No indeed. It is far more serious than that. We are telling the creator of the universe that He made a mistake, a substandard component when He chose to include them in his creative portfolio.

Now seriously contemplate this statement: Which of us in our right mind wants to confront the God of this universe face-to-face with that attitude? We, therefore, had better repent (change the way we think), get past this, all become one (John 17:21), and get focused on growing the spiritual kingdom so the King of All Glory can return (Matt. 24:14) and set up His physical kingdom (Ps. 2:6). And to cut to the chase, please employ the exhortation of a widely known, internationally advertised product, "Just do it!" Or perhaps you prefer, "Stop it right now!"

Okay, all together now. Let's all take three deep breaths. Slowly let each of them out.Then allow the inspiration of the Holy Spirit to infuse us with the mind of Christ and recite, "I will not ever again say, whisper, mutter, utter, or declare; neither will I entertain nor wink at this kind of ungodly conversation or thought because I choose to love every neighbor as myself and I am absolutely confident that you will enable me, Abba Father. And in Jesus's name, I declare it to be done. Thank You, Father. Amen (means let it be so).

Some acts of service just evoke such levels of joy that it is beyond my vocabulary to properly relate it, but here goes anyway. Our Friday night care group brainstormed and decided it to be worthwhile to begin to attempt to bring a measure of joy into the lives of the residents in our local nursing home. We were not exactly certain what to expect but were confident that something good would come of it. What we discovered when first we arrived was that many of the residents were slumped over in their wheelchairs or on their walkers. There were few smiles. Many were at the back of the very long room, eating their evening meal and obviously not at all interested in our presence.

But we were not to be discouraged and launched out with our offering of musical praise. Our orchestra, which was comprised of one acoustic guitar, and our choir, which consisted of some eight children and as many adults, launched into a joyful noise unto the Lord and continued with an offering of numerous choruses separated by verbal declarations of the goodness of God, His extravagant gift of His beloved son, and punctuated by the clapping of hands and expressive smiles fully loaded with cheer.

We soon noticed that some residents who were previously among those at the very back of the room had now, with the help of the nursing staff, made their way to the front. Some were now erect in their posture, a few were clapping in rhythm with the music, many were singing, and others were quite frankly, just observing the happenings.

As the evening progressed, it became apparent that the interest level had visibly increased, but the best part was yet to come. As we were about to verbalize the benediction, we advised the residents that the children had previously created handmade greeting cards and wished to share them with every resident who would care to receive one from one of the youngsters.

Well, you could just see the smiles and sense the elation from both women and men in the large room, and participation was widely evident. These young "ministers" were a smash hit, and the grand finale was quite unexpected and so welcome. As we announced our imminent departure, several of the residents began to shout their appreciation, and many additionally began to implore us to return again and wanted us to know that sooner was preferred to later.

We told them that we were most willing to return frequently and recommended that they ask the staff to have us return. There was much joy for each person of the praise team, both children and adult, but there was additionally a wonderful learning experience to be had. We discovered that there was a great chasm that had been vaulted during that hour and fifteen or so minutes. It became obvious that each of those residents had revisited some joy-filled childhood memories of a life that existed before the arrival of adulthood and its ensuing pressures and great demands, and if that were not enough, then came their advancing age, which brought further disappointment as they became unable to care for themselves. In many cases, their driving privilege had been suspended, and subsequently they were displaced from their home. And now far too many of them were infrequently visited by their children, who were now dealing with those same pressures and demands to which they had been previously subjected. But the good news is that we were to learn that we could be instrumental in helping them to hurdle over those difficult and very disappointing years by asking some seemingly childish or perhaps even silly questions. We asked them questions such as, "When you were growing up, what did you name your dolly? What was your favorite candy? What flavor of ice cream did you like the most? How old were you when you got your BB gun? Was the brand name of your first bicycle a Schwinn, a J.C. Higgins, or a Raleigh? What was the name of your best friend? What is your earliest childhood memory?"

As you quickly noticed, these are all questions designed to help transport them back to a time that is more likely to evoke fond memories. And an equally important lesson learned was that we can use similar questions when attempting to make new friends and when wishing to bring revival to the discouraged and downtrodden (Isa. 50:4-5) that are still at a considerable distance from the health care phase of advanced age.

The bottom line is that every single one of us is in a full-time business of service (call it good neighbor, or bond servant), and the most profound component of our daily activity is this: They (anyone with whom we come into contact) do not care what we know until they know that we care. Don't just go past this statement. Read it again and yet again. Then commit it to memory, and finally compare it to a familiar statement by our leader, "I have compassion on the multitude."

"They" are the multitude with which each of us comes into contact as we traverse our daily path. "They" are desperate for the answers to daily living that are to be provided by kingdom kids, those of us who are continuously connected to the power source (Acts 1:8) that have been made freely available to us by God the Father through the request of Jesus, the beloved Son (John 14:16–17, 26). We must learn to daily employ this compassionate (pity accompanied by tender affection) and caring approach. We should determine to make this our ongoing lifestyle, the starting point of our daily witness. Will we?

Earlier there was the brief mention that there are some actions we display that must be unlearned. Whether they were learned, adopted, or naturally (carnally) gravitated to is really irrelevant. It is certainly in our best interest to cease this sort of activity. Most of it occurs without our really realizing it. You know, it's as simple as a sneeze or a small tickle in the throat, and we touch our throat and say something like, "Sure hope I'm not coming down with a cold." Or perhaps there is a pain in our side, and we blurt out something akin to, "The last thing I need is appendicitis or a kidney stone. I cannot afford to miss work." And then we might even place the back of our hand to the center of our forehead to see if we can detect a fever. Or perhaps our child says, "Mommy, I have a really bad headache," and we turn to our friend and seemingly innocently say something like, "Almost every one of my brothers and sisters started out at a very young age with severe headaches, and I just hope that ..."

Well, you get the idea. Or your wife twists her ankle during a volleyball game, and you rush to her side and say something like, "Honey, you severely turned your ankle. Do you want me to take you to the emergency room?" Then there's the scenario where several things go wrong simultaneously, for example, the garbage disposal becomes clogged while you are cooking dinner and from the back room you hear a bloodcurdling scream from your youngest. And if that were not enough, the telephone suddenly rings, and you hear yourself saying, "I can't handle this. It's making me crazy." Or you're driving home from work and remembering that the automobile insurance renewal is due and the mortgage payment needs to be made. And you then hear a very loud and ominous sound coming from the engine compartment. And oh yes, the two front tires on your wife's vehicle are fast approaching the replacement stage, and your bank balance is far less than you want to recall. And now a guy in one of those high-lift dually pickups with a 250 pound bumper cuts you off in traffic, and you hear words like you would never want your family to hear, and they are coming off your lips.

Or similar frustrations of the day have worn you down, and you find yourself kicking the wall of the garage, slamming the kitchen cabinet door, pounding the steering wheel of the vehicle, or perhaps slamming the bathroom door, but at least in these instances you did not verbalize the intense aggravation that you experienced.

Well, here comes the series of questions that I wasn't excited to entertain, and they were not spoken to me via human communication: Is satan a created being? Are you a created being? Can you read the mind of another created being? Then is satan able to read your mind? So, if satan is unable to read your mind, then why in the world would you ever want to make negative declarations that will enable him to know exactly the types of pain, frustration, discomfort, aggravation, and unexpected occurrences of life that throw you into the abyss of despair?

So I then thought, "Well, if I just stop negative declarations, that alone will greatly reduce the ability of the enemy to plot and implement attacks upon me." Then another question was posed: As a created being, are you able to read the body language of another created being and detect anger, frustration, disappointment, dejection, fear, hopelessness, and such without him or her so much as speaking a word?

At this point, it becomes obvious to me. I am quite clearly my own worst traitor, and further, I must immediately begin to unlearn these weaknesses. Well, actually I need to renew my mind because, when I tolerate negativity by any expression, I am, innocently or not, agreeing with satan against God, which provides a portal of access to the evil one. By contrast, when I determine to deny this access to him, I can, at the least, frustrate his ability to readily torment me. And which of us can't see the obvious benefits of that? Hmm, please excuse me while I now internalize the merits of this realization. selah

One of the questions that seems to bring differing opinions is whether prayer for the healing of the unsaved is scriptural or even permissible. After all, Psalm 66:18 records,

" If I regard iniquity in my heart, The Lord will not hear." But as I begin to revisit the signs, wonders, and miracles demonstrated by our Lord, I can't recall even one instance where He instructed a person in need to fall down, worship Him, and ask for forgiveness of his or her sin before He would supply his or her need. Oh, I recognize that, in His early ministry, Jesus's mission field was to His own ("the lost sheep of the house of Israel")(Matt. 10:6) and that He described all of his works as "the children's bread" in his dialogue with the woman of Canaan, as recorded in Matthew 15:22-28.

Yet, even in this instance, He met the need of this outsider because of her great faith, humility, and persistence. It appears that her request fell within the parameters of Jesus's declaration in John 10:37-38, 14:10-11, where He stated essentially that, if you are unable to believe His words, then at least believe the works as proof that they manifest as a result of His relationship with the Father.

So then, if I am a born-again believer in Jesus and therefore am in relationship with the Father (John 17:20-21), does it not follow that, as one operating under the authority (*exousia*, Greek) of Jesus, I too can pray for any person who is in need of heavenly intervention? It now appears certain to me that I legally can, and indeed I shall! Come on, and join in. There is certainly a spot designed specifically for you.

Long have I followed with great interest the trek that Joseph took from his youth to Pharaoh's palace. The highs and lows of his life seemed to me to represent much of a parallel of the life of a follower of Christ with its ups and downs, its accompanying personal attacks, its being "in the pit," the false accusation, and the selling out to the enemy, but remaining faithful to God, ultimately reaching the palace of the most powerful leader on the planet, and then being elevated to a position second to him only in regard to the throne (Gen. 41:40b).

And by the way, you may recall another Bible character who, during a time of extremely difficult circumstances, was vaulted to a position that was second only to a most powerful king. Esther 10:3 records that Mordecai the Jew was also elevated second to powerful King Ahasuerus. Hold that thought just a moment, and recall that, in Genesis 1:26, God had determined to make man in His own image and after his likeness and to give him dominion (rulership) over everything on earth (except other humans, of course).

Then after man lost dominion, God came to earth in human form "to seek and to save" that which had been lost. Then fast-forward to a time yet to come when the King of Glory will return again to this planet and set up His physical kingdom (Psalm 2) on a newly created earth and will sit on King David's throne. I can't help but wonder. Did the psalmist David have this understanding when he penned Psalm 8:4-6, "For you have made him (man) a little lower than Elohim (Hebrew) ... You have made him to have dominion over the works of Your hands; you have put all things under his feet."

Just a little food for thought. Jesus seems to corroborate this in the parable of the talents in Matthew 25:21 and Luke 19:17. Might we not be "second to Him only in the throne"? After all, as believers, we are children of the Great King. What says the Holy Spirit to you concerning this possibility?

So what is the primary source of my diet of spiritual things? Where do I derive the majority of my nutrition? Do I look primarily or perhaps solely to other human teachers for my spiritual nourishment and sermon or teaching preparation? Many species of birds gather food for their young, chew it up, and then feed this regurgitation to their little ones. Not so the eagle. This high flyer that soars above the storms of life and renews its strength and youth, delivers only undigested food to its fledglings. Now, consider the result (Isa. 40:31b). Should I choose this as a model to follow in my approach to growth in kingdom understanding and living?

Oh, of course, there is much good information to be had from the scores of books to be found in the bookstores and libraries in this world; however, there is just one source that is not regurgitated but is "living" (John 6:63), only one that includes a "helper" that will guide me into all truth (John 16:13), and only one by which all others are to be measured. Thus, it seems logical to me that, if my wish is to soar above the storms of life and renew my strength and youth, my primary supply of spiritual nutrition should be pure, not regurgitated and directly from the original source.

The citizens of Berea (Acts 17:11b) clearly seem to have both learned and employed this necessity. I hear the prompting that it is okay to snack on the Spirit-led writings of man, but I should determine to feast upon every God-inspired word. What do you hear concerning this matter?

The author of the book of Hebrews has exhorted us to provoke (stir up) one another to love and good works (10:24). Recall this and couple with this scripture the fact that Jesus clearly declared in Matthew 22:35-40 that every one of the commandments could be encapsulated into just two, namely to love the Lord God with our entire being and to love our neighbor (those who are nearby) as much as we love ourselves. It seems clear that the motivating force behind all that we are expected to achieve is to be love. Perhaps, you are thinking, "So what's new? Everyone already knows that fact."

Okay, so let's just walk down that trail and do some personal inventory using scriptural teaching as our self-evaluating measuring stick of where we are at any given time. Shall we use some thought-provoking questions immediately followed by, say, six blank lines on which we can individually assess our present spiritual state and then, as per Habakkuk 2:2, to write what we, with heaven's enabling, purpose to do to achieve continuous, observable, and measurable growth.

Let's use a number from one to seven (with seven being the highest, that is, you have mastered this) to measure our present level of maturity and immediately follow that number with what step(s) we will employ to achieve growth in every area we dare to confront. Shall we increase the importance of this with each of us agreeing to accept as fact that the definition of insanity is to continue to do what we have always done and expect a different result?

Just a friendly reminder: these questions are not solely for your pastor or other members of the church staff. They are for every regenerated person among us. Ready?

1. Have I grown in intimacy with Christ through the person of the Holy Spirit in the past twelve months (Ps. 16:11, 46:10; Phil. 3:10; James 4:8a)? In what ways? If not, what's my plan?

_____

_____

_____

_____

_____

_____

2.  Do I ask the Holy Spirit for my specific assignment(s) every day? "And as you go" (Matt.10:7–8)?

 

---

---

---

---

---

---

3.  Is my service to God a job or far better, is it the result of an intimate spiritual relationship?

 

---

---

---

---

---

---

4. Who have I mentored today? This week? This month? This year? Last year?

_____

_____

_____

_____

_____

_____

5. When someone leaves my presence, what does he or she take with him or her? Is he or she encouraged, refreshed, revived, restored, renewed, or simply allowed to return to his or her current negative condition of emptiness, weightiness, disappointment, hopelessness, and lacking fulfillment?

_____

_____

_____

_____

_____

_____

6. Is the ultimate goal (John 17:4) continually before me? Isn't this my purpose?

_____

_____

_____

_____

_____

7. Am I asking God to bless what I am doing, or am I asking Him to direct me to do what He is blessing?

_____

_____

_____

_____

_____

8. Every single thing I do or say, what is my motive?

_____

_____

_____

_____

_____

_____

9. If I died today, what spiritual legacy would I leave?

_____

_____

_____

_____

_____

10. Do I primarily consume the Word that others regurgitate, or do I mostly ferret its truths for myself (Prov. 25:2)? Do I consistently study to show myself approved? (2 Tim. 2:15)

_____

_____

_____

_____

_____

_____

11. Who have I served today? Yesterday? The day before? Last week? Last month?

_____

_____

_____

_____

_____

12. If monetary resources nor any other roadblock existed, what would I be doing today to disciple all nations?

_____

_____

_____

_____

_____

_____

13. Do I realize and accept that the unsaved don't care what I know until they first know that I truly care…. about them?

_____

_____

_____

_____

_____

_____

14. What have I done today, yes, this very day-to increase the kingdom of God (Matt.24:14)?

_____

_____

_____

_____

_____

_____

15. Am I daily living out the exhortations of Matthew 6:33, 10:7-8; Mark 16:15-20; John 15:14; Romans 12:1-2; and 1 Timothy 2:1-2? Am I intentional in my efforts?

_____

_____

_____

_____

_____

_____

16. If Jesus came to the foot of my bed this very night and asked me what I have done with the time, talent, and treasure that has been given to me, how would I answer Him?

_____

_____

_____

_____

_____

17. Have I truly learned to love? Jesus said there is no greater love than to lay down one's life for his friends (John 15:12–13). What could happen if I loved Jesus as much as He loves me?
(I gave myself a score of barely one for number seventeen and am determined to grow daily with His help.)

_____

_____

_____

_____

_____

_____

18. If everyone in my church were just like me, what kind of church would my church be? Reread, please.

_____

_____

_____

_____

_____

_____

19. Would you even entertain the thought of praying for an obviously physically impaired person, unknown to you, with his or her permission while in a public place? Does recalling that Jesus consistently demonstrated this lifestyle serve to embolden you?

_____

_____

_____

_____

_____

20. What if you were accused of being a believer in, and follower of Jesus and were hauled into a courtroom for your witness? Would there be enough evidence to convict you?

_____

_____

_____

_____

_____

21. What if you learned that you had just one week to live? Or, even better, what if you lived each week as though it were your last?

_____

_____

_____

_____

_____

22. Do you intentionally seek out and draw into meaningful conversation persons who may not be seen as top tier? In fact, they may be seen as closer to invisible or perhaps wallflowers? How does heaven view them?

_____

_____

_____

_____

_____

_____

23. If God doesn't seem as close as He once did, guess who moved?

_____

_____

_____

_____

_____

_____

24. Do I anticipate with childlike enthusiasm the daily abiding in God's Word and my daily quiet time of intimacy with Jesus through the person of the Holy Spirit (Rev. 3:2)?

_____

_____

_____

_____

_____

_____

25. What occurs internally if someone takes my seat, parking place at church, or chair at work?

_____

_____

_____

_____

_____

_____

26. Am I celebrating my fellow man or am I just tolerating him?

_____

_____

_____

_____

_____

_____

Well, if you found yourself struggling with those twenty-six questions, don't feel alone. As was previously stated, the Holy Spirit can certainly provoke unto love and good works, but without Him we are assuredly certain to fail. My view of the lifestyle of a determined follower of the Lord is comparable to walking up a down escalator, that is, if you ever stop walking, you are certain to go backward. It happens so gradually that you hardly notice it at the beginning.

It's as though my soul were a pickup. if I just leave one shovelful of cow dung (representing sin) in the back of it, it only gives off a slight odor to which I can soon adapt; however, if the refuse continues to collect in the back, several negatives will occur. First, the stench will become blatantly offensive. Next the vehicle will become difficult to control, the fuel efficiency will be greatly reduced and, if allowed to continue, the springs, shock absorbers, and other body parts are certain to wear prematurely, leading to a most dangerous condition and, ultimately, total failure.

And friends, this is very much like what happens when an individual stops walking forward with the Lord through the person of the Holy Spirit. Sin begins to collect, and without repentance, your life is sure to become a downhill spiral, which most assuredly is likely to lead to predictable destruction. Consider the following example, please.

I declare to you that I have come to realize that you are my best friend and invite you on an extended journey. We load up in my vehicle, and shortly I turn on my CD player and begin to enjoy my favorites. After a bit, recalling that there are some potato chips in the floorboard behind me, I grab the bag and begin to munch a bunch. Time passes, and I decide to listen to an e-book on my tablet. And then after a while, I reach for the bag of sweets that were also on the floorboard next to the chips and proceed to partake of them. And then remembering that there also are several sodas, now I begin to imbibe. And later, determining that I am tiring of the plot of the e-book, I decide to listen to XM radio for the remainder of the journey while intermittently conversing with several fellow cellular phone owners.

Upon arrival at the somewhat lengthy destination, I turn to you and ask, "Well, what do you think?"

And you respond, "What do you mean what do I think? You led me to understand that I was your best friend, yet we travelled this great distance, and you did not speak to me or even consult with me one single time. And now that this extended journey is completed, you belatedly ask for my input?"

And here is the most disturbing part of this matter my friends. This is exactly what far too many of us do to the person of the Holy Spirit every single day of our lives. We take journeys day after day and do our own thing while so frequently we totally fail to consult the Holy Spirit and, as a result, grieve Him, completely disregarding that His mission is to come alongside (*paraclete*, Greek) to both comfort us and to lead us into all truth.

Such blatant disregard must not continue if we truly perceive Him to be our best friend; nor can we forget that Jesus returned to heaven and asked the Father (John 17) to send this most intelligent gift. (If He can guide us into all truth (John 16:13), He must have access to all knowledge required to direct us throughout our time upon this earth and empower us to achieve the fulfillment of our destiny that our Father had determined for us even before our birth was contemplated). C'mon, let's stop this foolishness and avail ourselves of the greatest power on earth.

Let's start today, even right now, and resolve to continue until Matthew 24:14 is completely fulfilled. Will you choose to accept, without further delay, the absolute necessity of such a change?

Perhaps you know someone that you want to enable to come into the full knowledge of the truth that Jesus is the only way to the Father (John 14:6). He or she tells you that he or she feels certain that Jesus is a prophet, a great teacher, or a good man, but in his or her mind, he or she is just as certain that He is not God. We realize that an argument or full-frontal confrontation inevitably results in a negative result and usually increases the likelihood that the next person who attempts to witness to such an individual will have an even greater possibility of failure.

This seems to be a real dilemma, but as usual, the answer is found in communicating via prayer to the heart changer. It seems that, when we are in a sleep state, we are unable to reject the downloading of a dream or vision that is activated within our brain. We can learn of this in God's library of love in Job 33:14-16. Just follow along and be prepared to get surprised. "For God may speak in one way, or in another, yet man does not perceive it. In a dream, in a vision of the night, when deep sleep falls upon men, while slumbering on their beds, then He opens the ears of men and seals their instruction."

So consider this. Why not remind the Father of His promise that He is not willing that any perish (2 Peter 3:9) and ask Him to provide the certainty that His Son is indeed God through a visitation by the person of the Holy Spirit, dream, or a vision or by opening his or her heart to receive your verbal witness? As I am sure you have already considered, this is also a wonderful method to employ to reach the closed ears of those in deceptive cults or false religion.

I do not mean to convey the idea that this method is in any way to be utilized as a substitute for my assignment to display a Christlike lifestyle on a daily basis, but I am also fully aware of the supernatural way that Jesus revealed Himself to Saul of Tarsus on the road to Damascus (Acts 9:1-9). And since He is no respecter of person (Acts 10:34), I feel confident He will entertain this request and will become fully engaged in the performance of it.

I have heard it said that, in any circumstance where we are desiring the best solution, we should write down up to ten possibilities that God could use to answer our dilemma. Then turn it over to Him, and be prepared to be astounded when He uses none of our ideas, but His is better than the sum total of all ours.

It seems certain that Isaiah 55:8-9 provides the solution, "'For My thoughts are not your thoughts, nor are your ways My ways,' says the Lord. 'For as the heavens are higher than the earth, So are My ways higher than your ways, and My thoughts than your thoughts.'" Isn't that the end of the matter?

Intimacy? Perhaps you have heard it described as "into me see" or "see into me." In any event, it defines a close friendship that is created through the transparency of both parties. It seems clear to me, for example, when my wife is attempting to begin a dialogue about the events of the day and I am oblivious. I am sitting in my chair with my favorite magazine, book, or newspaper in front of my face. The TV is on, and I obviously am not making eye contact. My response to her question, "What kind of day did you have, honey?" becomes something akin to, "Oh, the usual," "nothing special," or perhaps "same old stuff." It is patently obvious that I am not engaged and certainly am not even closely approximating a state of intimacy.

At a minimum, I should respect my soul mate enough to lower my reading material to my lap, mute the volume of the TV or preferably turn it off, look her in the eyes, smile, speak to her in a tender or gentle voice, and relate at least one event, good or not so good, that impacted my day. Far too few of us guys get it. We fail to observe the relationship between intimacy and love. And please, don't miss this. When we men choose to reveal our inner selves, it comes across as intimacy to those important ladies in our life, for example, our mothers, daughters, and absolutely our wives. (And a similar approach should, of course, be utilized by those singles among us toward those they hope will become their best friend and potentially future spouses.)

Our wives perceive that we men consider them to be significantly important enough in our life when we choose to demonstrate a willingness to share our innermost thoughts and experiences with them. Might this be a part of the meaning expressed in Genesis 3:16 where it is stated that a woman's desire shall be for her husband? And we can move it to a second level of intimacy when we choose to get out of our chair and move next to them, put our arm around them, and revisit a prior time we shared perhaps a special dining event, a memorable evening, an extended ride through the countryside, or one amazing event or photo that occurred during our wedding or the events leading up to the ceremony.

And you just have to consider this fact. There is an additional action that can unbelievably impact the level of intimacy in a relationship, but unfortunately it is rarely performed by us menfolk. Perhaps because we deem it an activity for the ladies; however, the simple fact that ladies see it as important should be a major clue for us guys to give it a wholehearted try.

Just pop in to the store, find the greeting card section, locate a card that most closely approximates feelings you can relate to, and then take the time to write in your own handwriting some special event that the two of you have shared. Now if you really want to make her day, do this on any day that is not her birthday, wedding anniversary, or Valentine's Day. No, not even Mother's Day. And if you really want to further escalate the value of this adventure, pick up one rose, take the card and the one rose home, sneak them in, put them in her favorite chair or on her pillow, and let her discover them.

Now the final topping on this gift is to buy two cards and give her the second card about fourteen or so days later. You won't be sorry, but you will be amazed. Just expect to find that she will keep the card(s), and you will quite possibly overhear her telling someone about this. It's an event that some folk have been known to refer to as "a random act of kindness."

But know this: what you have just achieved is far greater than the mere fact of the act of buying a card and a rose. No, indeed. You have chosen to celebrate her, a thoughtful act with long-lasting implications.

I now feel compelled to address the following. Please don't make the mistake of thinking me to be some kind of genius at this sort of behavior. Trust me. It is a learned response that has occurred over an extended period of time. Metamorphosis takes a very long time. In my case it has already taken more than sixty years, and my sincere prayer is that you are teachable and a quicker study than I have proven to be.

So this very morning, I elected to poke around Cindy's bedside table and, in the process, discovered three greeting cards I had given her within the last year, but further sleuthing revealed many more in her secret stash that covered a span of several years.

Please allow me to reveal my both secret and primary source of this extended metamorphosis. You see, it's all about love, but perhaps not at all how men we perceive it. Oh, I think most of us guys recognize that the ladies are repositories of love, right? And as such, their love container needs continuous refilling, agreed? But the problem surfaces when we males find it difficult (perhaps next to impossible) to adequately supply the requisite quantities needed to maintain this incomparable wellspring that assures joy-filled living.

Just check this out. Our inability to meet this genuine need actually stems from our poor maintenance of or, even worse, a perhaps, totally nonexistent yet entirely separate relationship. By now, you may be thinking, "Whoa, dude, you have really lost it. You have simply gone way too far with this."

But please, just hang with me a bit longer. So before we can determine where we want/need to go (like using a G.P.S.), we must first know our current location, agreed? Okay, can we now agree that we feel inadequate to supply this seemingly insatiable appetite? All right, can we also now recognize/admit that, since we are inadequate to meet this existing and essential need, we should first locate and then consistently maintain an inexhaustible source of supply from which we may draw? And, oh yes, can we further recognize that, when we locate a needed source of supply for archery, bodybuilding, bowling, camping, fishing, hunting, running, tennis, and the like, that there is typically an expert available who can prove invaluable to advise us in our quest for an upgrade?

Well, as for me, when I determine to take on a new pursuit, I choose not to reinvent the wheel, but rather to seek out those in the know. And that includes finding an expert who has considerable hands-on experience. Book knowledge alone just won't meet my expectation, and anyway it seems likely that this approach could as well prove helpful in shortening that learning curve scenario. I'm also thinking it takes several times longer to unlearn/relearn than it does to learn correctly from the outset. So if I'm to learn golf from an expert, I should expect to invest considerable one-on-one time with him, right? I tend to become more like those with whom I associate the most. Isn't that correct? And I don't want to develop poor habits that would have to be relearned. Thus it would be most beneficial to do only what he does, and to accomplish this, it becomes necessary to learn to think like he thinks.

Wow, it quickly becomes obvious that this is going to take a substantial as well as a long-term investment in time and determination, a genuine commitment to the entire process. It's certain that there will be stiff winds with which to contend, water hazards to be overcome, sand traps to frustrate me, people along the way to delay my progress, and my own emotional upheavals that are certain to be detrimental to my finishing the course.

Oh my, it has now become so obvious how absolutely essential it is for me to choose the most qualified expert for the task at hand. A wrong choice of an expert is certain to further complicate those intrinsic challenges that are previously listed, but equally of concern is the certainty of the consequences that are sure to occur should I choose not to follow his tried and proven direction.

And so where do I begin? While experience can prove valuable, it is well understood that years alone do not an expert make. So then I suppose it would prove wise to research the track record of the expert who is under consideration and not simply accept what he or she claims for himself or herself, but also include in the mix what others say about results achieved during their relationship with this self-proclaimed expert. I understand that this step is so obviously crucial in this decision-making process; however, I am just as certain that it is all too frequently overlooked.

How many of us have fallen prey to persons simply because they looked or smelled good or seemed right or some other such stimulus? Far too many, I perceive. So then, positive results achieved over an extended period of time would seem to be the preferred method of determining which candidate to choose. And as I begin to contemplate this parcel of information, my thoughts go to my life history, which I have come to call my rearview mirror. It then becomes readily apparent that my life has been crafted, directed, and enabled by one who is an expert in absolutely every microcosm of every life that has existed since the dawn of man, including mine.

Yes, "omniscience" is the word of choice to describe this awesome entity that has declared Himself to be identified as "I am who I am," the eternal, self-existent one. Yes, the one whose fundamental characteristic and essence is love (1John 4:8, 16) and who loves me with an undying love. So it now is so obvious that He is my expert who desires to enable me to dispense such insatiable appetites for love. So if I now recognize that I am unable to adequately supply this request in my own strength, I require an expert to enable me to meet this request. And I further realize that I become like those with whom I regularly associate. Isn't it logical to conclude that I am not yet spending the requisite time in the presence of the expert who will assure the ability to maintain an adequate supply?

Suddenly I hear, "husbands, love your wives" (Eph. 5:25) ringing in my ears. Please excuse me for a while. My expert is calling. I will return when this episode of my education has been learned. Care to join this counseling session?

In approximately April 2002, I was traveling Interstate 10W from Seguin to my job in San Antonio. I consistently used this forty-minute drive on I-10 to be a time of prayer, praise, singing, worship, and intimacy with the Lord and made it a matter of habit not to even play the radio nor do anything that might become a distraction. Of course, my eyes were constantly open as I traveled, despite knowing that he gives His angels charge over me.

On this particular morning while in a state of worship and driving in the inside lane closest to the center median, my attention was drawn to a vehicle on my right side that was even with my vehicle. I felt a sudden urgency to immediately slow my vehicle so that the auto on my right would move ahead of me. I had no sooner done this when that vehicle turned sharply across my path, violently drove into the center median area, and lost partial control of the vehicle while turning 180 degrees. And then within a few seconds, it skidded to a complete stop. I watched in my rearview mirror until certain that the vehicle remained upright and then realized with absolute certainty that I had just been the recipient of heavenly favor through the warning of the person of the Holy Spirit.

What I was to later learn from Cindy was that, within ten minutes after I had departed for work that day, she heard an inner voice that said to her that she had better have enjoyed what she had experienced during our two-plus years of marriage as it was about to be over (coming to an end). She began to immediately intercede in prayer, claiming the essence of results promised in Psalm 145:18-20 to wit, "The Lord is near to all who call upon him, to all who call upon Him in truth. He will fulfill the desire of those who fear him; He also will hear their cry and save them. The Lord preserves all who love Him, but all the wicked He will destroy."

There is no doubt whatsoever in our collective hearts that heaven through the cooperation of the Holy Spirit and very possibly the efforts of guardian angels (Ps. 91:11) was fully engaged in the protective early warning shield of the Holy One of Israel. I just know one inarguable certainty: God's love (Strong's Concordance: H5689, G25) for me is immeasurably more vast and powerful than satan's hatred of me, and that is a comforting truth that no quantity of treasure or effort could ever purchase. We must permanently settle this matter in our heart, which means that, no matter the perceived gravity of any event in our life, we must approach it, then confront it, and with total confidence know in our heart that, the greater the threat, the more extravagant the forthcoming heavenly solution is certain to be.

And this truth requires that we allow our deep (the deepest part of our soul) to cry out to the deep of His love while fully expecting that the immeasurable potency of His aga'pe is more than enough (omnipotent) for any set of circumstances that may appear on our horizon. Mil gracias, Señor. (That's Spanish for "A thousand thanks, Lord.")

You perhaps have heard it said regarding a tombstone that there are three important pieces of information to be considered: the birth date, the death date, and the space of time between those two. It's very much a given that the length of time in between is ultimately the most significant since it represents the achievements of the person whose name is inscribed on the stone. One thing that is not readily detectable is a list of all the significant events that occurred during the lifespan of that individual represented by the headstone. Thus we are unable to examine the value of any contributions made during the course of that life. However, we can be certain of one most sobering assurance, the life of that individual will be evaluated, and a just determination will occur in the courts of heaven as to what rewards, if any, will be forthcoming.

Recall with me, if you will, those extremely significant and telling words, "I have fought the good fight, I have finished the race, I have kept the faith. Finally, there is laid up for me the crown of righteousness, which the Lord, the righteous judge, will give to me on that Day, and not to me only but also to all who have loved His appearing" (2 Tim. 4:7-8). When I consider fighting well and finishing well, I can't help but think of a prize that could await me, you know, perhaps a trophy that represents a constant, ongoing, and growing effort and determination to finish well. Then as I consider the physical expenditures needed to fight well and to finish well, I am led to consider the alternative results, should I fail to continue to grow.

When I fail to exercise my body, it will weaken and not enable me to either fight or finish well. And when I relate this to my spiritual life, I can expect the exact same result. If I accept Jesus as my personal Savior, I have made a good start. If, however, I then fail to continue to make an ongoing effort to increase my strength and endurance through prayer, study of the Word, and intimate relationship with Him (which would assure my ability to learn to love Him more and to love others just as much as I love myself), I can fully expect to experience atrophy.

Did you notice? Just as between the birth and death dates on the headstone there is the space, there is also the difference of the space between atrophy and a trophy. The question that comes to mind seems to be: with what will I choose to fill that space? selah

A paradox exists that deserves our very best consideration, and that is this. My greatest strength can actually prove to be my greatest weakness and thus the largest impediment to the fulfilling of my heavenly assigned destiny. If, for example, my greatest strength is organization, preaching, or teaching, the charisma attached to that gifting can actually override my necessity to rely upon a heaven-driven heart to achieve the desired end result. My human abilities can only carry me so far and for a limited duration. It is essential therefore that all of my activities are drawn from a source that never runs dry and one that provides every facet needed to assure throne room results.

Let's face it. If lesson preparation comes easy to me, if delivery of that information flows well, and if I am well-rehearsed, blessed with great recall, and able to deliver it with gusto, my human tendency is to gravitate to an ever-increasing use of my own inherent abilities and to gradually diminish my dependence upon stimulus that can only be derived through an ongoing intimate relationship with an entity that is assuredly wiser, purer, and more powerful, one whose essence is an eternal love, certainly of unquestionable character, and ever available, just to name a few.

And without this input (anointing), attrition will ensue, and I will begin to have thoughts about how well I am personally performing, which thought life will drive my actions. And as time passes, I will develop habits based on my human tendencies, and these human stimuli will form my character that will determine my lifestyle, which ultimately is sure to have an adverse effect on my ability to achieve my God-designed and ordained destiny.

And the most worrisome part of all is that this can happen so gradually that it is very nearly imperceptible, that is, until it all comes crashing down. And the fact is, if we determine to do kingdom work in our own strength and abilities, we are setting ourselves up for certain failure.

And folks, it makes absolutely no difference whether we are a mentor of one, a small group leader of twelve souls, or pastor of a mega church of twelve or twenty thousand. Jesus declared in John 5:30, "I can of myself do nothing. As I hear, I judge; and my judgement is righteous, because I do not seek my own will but the will of the Father who sent me." How could you or I possibly expect to succeed with any different approach? Such arrogance is an affront and an insult to the Father and to His Son of whom He said, "This is my beloved son in whom I am WELL pleased."

This is one of those certainties that is best described as "the awful truth." These types of exceedingly uncomfortable admissions continue to present themselves as blatantly intolerable until a conscious decision is made to examine and discover the intrinsic value of such truth and a subsequent choice is made to appropriate it. And finally I must accept the fact that no one else can make these types of difficult choices for me. Since I have been afforded free moral agency, it is ultimately my decision to make. Ouch, here we grow again!

Learn something new every day! That's what Cindy said to me. As I contemplated the scope of this succinct challenge emanating from inside me, I heard the words, "As a man thinks in his heart, so is he." And then recalling that I had some seventeen years before tagged myself as the "world's oldest teenager," it became obvious to me that keeping my memory sharp and my learning faculties at the cutting edge was indeed an invaluable and necessary goal.

Considering that my seventy-fourth birthdate would soon arrive, it became obvious that sooner was a better choice than later. I also knew that an exercise regimen was an ongoing necessity, and some friends had on more than a few occasions suggested that golf could be a possible consideration to achieve both goals. Also observing that Cindy had decided to learn Spanish seemed to be a great opportunity for me to brush up my waning grasp of it at the same time. Sudoku, crossword puzzles, and Cryptoquips in the newspaper and consistent feasting in God's library of love had been my mainstay for years, so it wasn't necessary to start at ground zero. But increased activity should prove to be of considerable value. And further remembering that a young man in his twenties had recently informed me that he was praying to the Lord that my life would continue to age 130 so I could mentor his grandchildren added imperativeness to my decision to upgrade both my learning and exercise regimen since I have absolutely no intention of using even one man-made ambulatory device in my future.

And should the Lord direct that additional tomes, epistles, or greeting cards be written by my hand, it is necessary that my mind remain clear and sharp so the still, small voice will be spiritually perceived and accurately conveyed according to His direction.

They are all just a bunch of hypocrites. Why in the world should I even consider going to church? Have you ever heard, thought, or, for that matter, perhaps even made such a statement? I personally think this is a totally accurate observation and declaration and as such is deserving of our full and honest consideration. At this point, you may be thinking something akin to, "Surely, he just has to be kidding."

Please, just hop in the bus, and let's go down this road a little way. First, I recall reading that it's not good for man (mankind) to be alone. I recognize the context in which this scenario was written; however, when I continue to read to Genesis 3:8, there is incontrovertible proof that the Creator Himself thought it proper and necessary to be where his kids were. And recalling that He made us in His image and likeness (Gen. 1:26-27), it seems to me that this broader understanding merits our consideration as well.

And besides, there are those negative words like lonely, lonesome, loneliness, and, of course, alone, not to mention recluse and the memory of folks like aircraft magnate Howard Hughes and more recently actor Robin Williams that typify that lifestyle. The stories about such loners are replete with sour consequences and often surrounded with heartbreaking conclusions.

So on a personal level, have you ever gone to bed with the lights turned off and your mind begins to review the events of recent days, weeks, months, and perhaps even years? And you find yourself disappointed, abused, aggravated, anxious, fearful, bored, unfulfilled, unappreciated, disrespected, shunned, belittled, uncertain, and, perhaps worst of all, hopeless. And as a result, you discover that you are angry, bitter, morose, vengeance-seeking, retribution-desiring, and hate-filled and now considering doing things you would never before even have entertained in your thought life, let alone would you have begun to formulate some potentially awful actions that you could now consider justified in undertaking?

Well, here is the fact about this scenario. Those hypocrites in church are struggling with issues just as you are, but your issues and theirs may differ in that you struggle with anger and they may not. And they may have a lust issue, and you do not. Thus, you can be strong for them in their area of weakness, and they can be encouraging for you in yours. The present difference is that they have determined that they are unable to do it alone.

Just check this out. Basketball great Earvin "Magic" Johnson's coach could tell him what needed to be done, but the coach could not do it for him. Magic had to expend the requisite hours, days, weeks, months, and years to achieve the excellence to which he aspired and fully achieved.

Now consider this, if you have a problem with anger, lust, pornography, road rage, jealousy, shoplifting, illegal drug usage, alcohol abuse, gossip, adultery, or murder (as in your heart, you wish your boss, coworker, spouse, or some other person were dead), would you make a Paul Revere-style proclamation for all the world to know? If not, why would you expect those hypocrites at church to do so? You may already know that the word "hypocrite" conveys the meaning of wearing a mask to disguise who you really are.

So how do you respond when asked, "How's it going?" Do you freely admit that you think your child is on drugs, you think your spouse is cheating on you, there is more month than there is money, or you wish your boss were dead? Probably not, and neither do those hypocrites at church. But by becoming a part of a church family, they learn they are not alone in this complex world of trouble (John 16:33). And after having developed a relationship with others like themselves and utilizing biblical principles to change their manner of thinking (Rom. 12:2), they can become empowered to overcome the frequent treacherous events of daily living that are so prevalent in this present fallen world.

Hey, folks, it is truly a considerable comfort to become a regular attendee of a care group in your local congregation and to begin to cultivate friendships and then have someone in whom you can confide when you need comfort during those times when life deals you another of those predictable nasty blows. Are you familiar with the declaration that no man is an island?

And one final and most significant thing, those hypocrites are not the standard by which life is measured. His name is Jesus, and He was in all points tempted as we are. And He did not make a poor choice, not even once (Heb. 4:15). So please come on and join us hypocrites. We pledge to encourage you as together we travel the Romans 12:2 road on an ongoing basis. Be real now. You know you really want some comforting.

John the Beloved is my favorite apostle. There, I've said it and don't apologize for having said it. But please know that considerable thought, study, and prayer has preceded this declaration. Like so very many before me, I had considered the possibility that John could be considered to be a bit arrogant in his declared presumption that he was "the beloved." Also there was the consideration of his youthfulness. He asked the Lord whether it would be allowable to call down fire from heaven on those persons outside their group that were also performing great works. And then of course, the episode concerning whether he and his brother could be allowed to be seated on the left and right of the Lord when He came into His kingdom.

It would be greatly appreciated if you would permit me to share a portion of my thought process that brought me to such an overt conclusion. As a review of the scripture in John 13:22-25 transpired, it intrigued me that John could seemingly so easily move from reclining on Jesus's bosom to leaning on His breast, that is, until I remembered that, in the Middle East culture of that time, the table at which they were gathered was not as painted by Leonardo da Vinci in that classic painting of the Last Supper. No indeed, the table would have been round or square and approximately twelve inches above the floor. The disciples would have perhaps been sitting on pillows or reclining on their one elbow while accessing their food with their free hands. This posture would have enabled John to be immediately adjacent and abutted to Jesus and therefore effortlessly move from bosom to breast.

Two more things that occur to me are that, first of all, these twelve guys were not wimps. And yet that did not deter John from placing himself in a position that could certainly have been determined to be a step taken by a teacher's pet. But then after noting that Peter (most certainly a man's man) had motioned to John to ask the Lord of whom He spoke, it seemed to me that this was, at a minimum, a recognition by Peter that John had enough favor with the Lord to be comfortable to ask. And it seems to me to also be a demonstration of respect from Peter toward John. And further, after recognizing that the bosom is representative of security and closeness that can be likened to being held in a warm, familial embrace and that the breast is understood to be the seat of affection and emotion, it seems as well to me that John wanted to hear the heartbeat of God and clearly did not care what others thought about that choice. It is somewhat reminiscent of Mary's posture when Jesus came to visit (Luke 10:25) and she chose to sit at Jesus's feet and hear His words. And Jesus stated that Mary had chosen that good part.

I can't help but notice that John's choice very well might have come into play at the foot of the cross (John 19:26-27) when Jesus entrusted his mother's future care and well-being to John. And we would do well to remember that this act occurred in a culture that celebrated parental honoring and provision throughout their senior years (their "social security," if you will). It further seems probable to me that John might have called himself beloved because he knew beyond any doubt that he absolutely was loved.

I can't help but wonder if his great love for Jesus played a part in his being allowed to pen the gospel of John, three epistles, and the book of the Revelation of Jesus Christ. It's quite clear to me that John had a sure understanding of the essence of God when he recorded twice in 1 John 4:8, 16 that God is love, and certainly the powerful 1 John 3:1 recording. And, oh yes, we must never forget that one pivotal verse recorded in John 3:16, "For God so loved the world ... that He gave ... His most indescribably, extravagant gift (paraphrase is mine)."

Indeed, not only did John know about the love of God, he personally knew the God who is love. My heartfelt prayer is that we all, every one of us, come to this pivotal and crucial understanding as well. And further, that we proceed to walk it out as the central component in our ongoing lifestyle. This decision of attachment to The Vine (John 15:5) is certain to produce luscious first-fruit and in great abundance.

Family. Just how important is it anyway? Have you taken the time to give it a fair evaluation? It's rather obvious that Jehovah considered it to be of paramount importance. After all, it was the very first institution that He created. And He didn't just establish it and then move on. No he talked to Adam and Eve and instructed them to be fruitful and multiply.

Then He added further value to it by commanding that their issue were to honor their father and mother if they wished to live extended lives (Ex. 20:12). Let's just consider this, it seems we have lost our way in this crucial part of our daily living. When I volunteered to become a male guide (mentor) at the South Texas Pregnancy Care Center in Seguin I was shocked to find that most of the males that accompanied the young pregnant girls were also children themselves. In so very many instances both male and female were well below the ages of twenty. As I revisited my own maturity level at age 20 and earlier, I recalled so many more poor choices and decisions than I wanted to admit or confront. Nevertheless, it was an unarguable fact. I was just simply too unwise and inexperienced to determine my own path, let alone the paths of innocent babes and children, those invaluable treasures of which Jesus declared "Let the little children come to me, and do not forbid them; for of such is the kingdom of heaven." And please notice that these words of Jesus were recorded in all three of the synoptic gospels adding even greater significance to these little ones. Did you get that? Jesus, who only did and said what He saw and heard from the Father was saying that only those who will come to Him with childlike faith and are trusting, open to spiritual matters, tender, and hence vulnerable to mistreatment can expect to be permitted to enter into the kingdom of heaven. And since our Heavenly Father was so involved in the activity of children, I asked Him where humanity had gone wrong. I clearly heard that I was to ask each young man how he and his earthly father interacted. The first that I asked said his father left before he was born, the second replied that his father left when he was a few months old, the third stated that his had departed when he was 6 years of age, and the fourth responded that his dad was still at home, but then followed with the comments that he never talked to me or played "pitch and catch" etc. He went on to say he comes home, eats supper, watches TV, and drinks beer until bedtime and that is his daily practice. I wish I could tell you that reports like these were minimal, the fact ; however, is that they are a troublesome condition, not isolated circumstances. So we have children who have little or no knowledge of their Heavenly Father, no relationship with their earthly father and a young mother often raised in a similar environment and these two are making uninformed decisions for God's most precious creation. What believers in Christ can and MUST do is to become involved in the lives of their children and grandchildren, become active in the childrens ministry of a Bible-based Church and become volunteers in activities that invest in the lives of children and begin to mentor these treasures from heaven. Rest assured that we will give an answer as to what we did to rescue these precious gifts. We must remember that this cosmos is changed by Christ Followers who show up! Get immersed and involved. selah

There has been for a very long time some considerable questioning about the significance of the Christ's works, wonders, and miracles and, most certainly, as to whether they are relevant today. As always, it seems that going to the source is the best place to begin. Shall we just begin with what the Master Teacher said about them? On more than one occasion, He stated clearly, if they wouldn't believe His words, then His works should be accepted (John 10:38, 14:11), and that fact is sufficient for me.

But the place that impacts me the most is the occasion where John the Baptist is in prison. And having heard of the works of Christ, he then dispatches two of his disciples to ask Jesus if He is the coming one or should they look for another (Matt. 11:2–6).

In Luke's account of this same event (Luke 7:18-23), it seems obvious that the Lord makes it inarguably clear that His works are so much a necessary part of His ministry by demonstrating them in "that very hour" to "many" recipients (Luke 7:21). And as a footnote, please observe that the sequence was (Jesus's own words in Luke 7:22) that the works were performed first. And then he stated that "the poor have the gospel preached to them." It seems that He felt it advantageous, if not necessary, to take care of their physical condition prior to addressing their spiritual need.

Please just consider this. Am I more likely to be able to fully concentrate on your message if my head or other body parts are not causing me pain or aggravation?) And recalling that He only did/said what He observed the Father doing/ saying (John 5:19, 30), it seems certain this was Father-directed. So isn't it likely that people are better prepared to hear spiritual matters after their physical matters have been addressed? Just asking, it seems likely.

And as to the issue of whether those same works and miracles are still appropriate, it seems necessary to consider His omniscience, compassion, and the stated fact that He is no respecter of person. Consider please that He has knowledge of all that will occur throughout the entirety of time (Isa. 42:9). This assures us that He was fully cognizant of all the diseases (AIDS, arthritis, cancer, carpal tunnel syndrome, cystic fibrosis, Parkinson's, lupus, diabetes, Ebola, fibromyalgia, PTSD, and so on) and countless dilemma that would come on the earth after the time of the twelve apostles.

We need only revisit the contents of Matthew 24, Mark 13, and Luke 21 to settle that fact. And since He is the same yesterday, today, and forever (Heb. 13:8), it seems certain that He continues to have compassion on the multitude. Can we truly believe that He was more caring of those who were suffering then than those who suffer today? That wouldn't be love nor justice would it? When we begin to insert kingdom thinking (Matt. 6:33), we are better able to understand this issue. God is a righteous king. As such, He is fully determined to supply all our need (Phil. 4:19) from His inexhaustible supply. We need only to accept Him as our King and believe that He can and will freely provide all our need. We need only to observe an earthly kingdom, such as seen in Great Britain to see that there are various departments of ministry that are specifically determined to meet the needs of the kingdom subjects (the citizenry). And when a ministry leader dies, the department does not cease to exist. No, the highest level of the kingdom then appoints an appropriate replacement. And when we come to understand this concept, we can fully grasp the certainty that, when the original twelve apostles died, they were replaced by qualified, kingdom-appointed ambassadors (2 Cor. 5:20) who were endowed with the same level of government undergirding (Isa. 9:6-7) as those that preceded them.

This is to say that every sincere believer in Christ Jesus the Lord can fully expect and further has a responsibility to, both appropriate and demonstrate the works that Jesus Himself did because Jesus Himself stated that the works He did and greater than those would be done by His kingdom kids (Gen.1:26-27; Mark 16:16-20; John 14:12).

Consider, if you will, the handiwork of the Great King. A wonderful demonstration of this occurs during the six days of creation when every single item of mankind's physical need was supplied before man was created. Just a point to ponder. Shouldn't we just pause and prayerfully examine this. Come on now. May we reason together? Let's not limit our conclusion to the comments of men. Let's base our determination on the words and wondrous acts of the beloved Son of God. selah

Do you frequently find yourself separated from others? Have you on more than a few occasions felt lonely even in a crowd? Do you choose to distance yourself from meaningful dialogue? Is it your preference to be apart from even those of your own approximate age? Have you ever thought you'd be at least as well off to be alone on an otherwise uninhabited island? Do you feel that you have nothing to offer? Does it seem to you that people don't even notice you or that anything you have to say appears to be of no importance to them? Have you ever felt that it seems as though even God seemingly isn't aware of your existence?

Well, my friend, there is good news for you to consider. You have been tricked, deceived, lied to, misled, and duped! Right about now, you may possibly be thinking or even saying, "You have no idea what my life has been like, including right up to this very moment."

Bingo! Jackpot! You are 100 percent correct. I have absolutely no clue. There exists, however, a parcel of information that I would strongly encourage you to evaluate. The bad news is that it requires effort, determination, and even a conscious decision on your part to begin to walk a path that will change this present dilemma. The great news is that it not only can be done, but even better, you can have a partner who will walk every single step with you. And further, it will even help you get back on your feet when you slip or, heaven forbid, should you inadvertently fall (Ps. 37:23–24).

Are you interested? I was reasonably certain that you might be. And, oh yes, it makes no difference whether you are male or female. You might think, "Yeah right, my family has little or no social status, and I would be likely to be voted as least likely to succeed even by my own family members." Or you may think, "Additionally party invitations and such celebrations never find their way to my mailbox." You continue, "I don't see myself as having even one person that I can confidently call a friend. As a result, social skills are certainly not at an appreciable level on my relational resume'. I don't view myself as particularly attractive, I can't play a musical instrument, I have no propensity toward any sports activity, or I am certainly not a public speaker and do not have the confidence to attempt to become one."

My friend, you are not the first; nor will you be the last to entertain such thoughts. Self-evaluations like these have existed for thousands of years. One such occurrence is recorded in the book of Judges chapter 6, a book that was recorded a thousand years before Jesus's earthly visit. Check out Gideon (Jerubbaal) beginning at Judges 6:11 and take particular notice of Judges 6:15. Sound familiar?

But do yourself a favor. Read on and give utmost attention to Judges 6:12, 16. Did you notice the promise that the Lord made in Judges 6:16, "Surely I will be with you." That very promise extends to you since we know that God is no respecter of persons (Acts 10:34) "Yes, you say, "but I'm a girl, and girls aren't always valued as highly as males. What about me?"

Let's take a trip and visit a girl who lived at least four hundred years before Jesus's time on earth. She was without father or mother and raised by her cousin, not really an auspicious beginning, especially when we observe that she was also a captive in a foreign land, which further reduced the likelihood of her rising out of her circumstances.

Shall we pick up the story of Hadassah in Esther 2:7 and observe how her life was directed or choreographed, if you will? And by an amazing set of events, this young woman made herself available, teachable, and willing, so she could enable her entire nation to escape total annihilation despite the fact that they were seemingly at the mercy of one of the most powerful kingdoms on the earth. Just consider the extraordinary courage that Hadassah (Esther) displayed, and recall that she was able to rise incredibly further from her beginning circumstances than any person might expect.

And if your great concern is your youthfulness, let's inspect the passage recounted in the book of Jeremiah beginning in the very first chapter, especially Jeremiah 1:4–8, where God assures Jeremiah that He will deliver him regardless of his youth or his circumstances. So be encouraged, and starting this very day, rest assured that your creator only makes originals. And know that, just as there are no two snowflakes that are exactly the same, the same can be said of you. There has never been; nor will there ever be another human just like you. You absolutely are one of a kind. The Father only creates originals. Come on now. Start today with a daily dose of God's library (The Holy Bible, His constitution, His covenant; His law).

And begin to fill your mind, soul, spirit, and heart with His inarguable promises as to who you are in Him. Then set aside a specific time to be alone with Him daily. Next approach Him with a gentle, tender, loving heart, and ask Him to speak clearly into your spirit with His incessant reminders as to who and what you are to Him. You can be absolutely certain that your new path (Ps. 16:11) will become a joyride that will far exceed what your eye has ever seen, what your ear has previously heard, or what your mind can even imagine (1 Cor. 2:9). Next, begin to look for a person who seems to represent the old you, and demonstrate your new lifestyle to him or her so he or she is able to access this same joy-filled existence that you have newly discovered. And guess what? You now have a friend with which to share, and you need never be lonely again. Perhaps the two of you could duplicate this event with two other loners? A brand new small group! What a wonderful difference that would make! And you should recall that what a person sows, that shall they also reap (Gal. 6:7-9). Today could very well be the perfect day to start this new endeavor. Bon voyage. Godspeed!

Some of my favorite people on the planet are youth and children. They are wonderful examples of joy, expectation, and celebration, and for the most part, they are not yet laden with the garbage that life can heap upon mankind. They can still go about life with a song in their heart and a hum in their throat, and some of them even know how to deliver a whistle from their lips. All of this is a wonderful certainty that they have not succumbed to the maladies of living, but rather they are still led by the melodies that erupt from their heart. They often express a seemingly impossible dream that is stirring about within them.

A youngster may confidently declare, "Mom, I want to become the president of the United States."

All too often, we squash that declaration with words like, "Oh, honey, that is just not going to happen, so forget it."

I often wonder what would happen if instead we joyfully exclaimed what a wonderful goal that is and told the child that we have much preparatory growth to achieve and knowledge to acquire. That is, we need to explore the different cultures throughout the world, we must develop a powerful command of language to include learning multiple languages, we need to learn debating skills, our technology skills must be highly developed, we must learn to fully develop our relational skills, and certainly we must study government.

In short, we address such lofty dreams with a can-do approach and greatly encourage the child or youngster to begin to formulate and write down his or her vision (Hab. 2:2) so he or she can follow it to an excitingly fruitful conclusion.

First of all, who am I to presume that God has not placed such an amazing dream in the heart of one of His favorite created beings (Matt. 19:13-15)? And even if that particular dream does not unfold, would it be so terrible if the child develops into a neurosurgeon, an author, a philanthropist, a CEO of an international corporation, or an educator with a penchant for developing our children and youth into becoming what they genuinely desire to become?

I understand that the high school coach of NBA legend Michael Jordan told him that he would not become a major player in basketball. I wonder how many similar declarations have shattered dreams. I am personally committed to encourage every, single, so-called crazy dream, by encouraging each carrier of such dreams to formulate a plan and to advise him or her to do it while seeking advice, knowledge, and wisdom from the repository of all such needed information. He is to be discovered in the writings of Isaiah 55:1-13, a chapter devoted to the development of an abundant life.

Would you please join me in becoming an encourager of such? After all, we are talking about the future of a once-great, God-loving nation that can return again to Him and effect a renaissance (Isa. 43:18-19) of relationship at a level not yet attained by any previous generation. It only takes three to get this done: you, me, and He (the King of Glory). I'm quite certain it's His dream and that He is engaged. Do you have vision for this? Let's change the motto of "God bless America" into "America, bless God!" The visionaries among us deserve such an environment in which to thrive without restriction.

It was a typical day in small town America, and the pantry was nearing bare so a quick trip to WalMart seemed in order. I puttered down the aisles, found all my needs, and, verifying I qualified for the less than twenty-item maximum, headed for the quick check cashier. My preferred one offers a clear view into the optical center where my beloved plies her trade.

No sooner had I placed my first item on the countertop when I clearly heard within, "Talk to her."

Internally, I heard myself thinking "What"?

And again the words "Talk to her" echoed from within.

Being one of those who has never met a stranger, out popped those intellectually stimulating words, "Howzit goin'?"

She responded, "Oh, fairly well."

Discerning a tone of reticence, I reloaded with an additional powerful query, "Really?"

Detecting that there was more than polite interest in her present circumstances, she continued with, "I'm concerned about my daughter, and I will be taking her to the doctor for a checkup when I go off duty today. It seems she may have contracted something while in the hospital."

Internally the words surfaced, "Pray with her."

My thoughts went to, "Gladly, Lord, but you will have to keep this line empty of anxious shoppers."

Folks, if you have ever utilized the quick check in any store, especially Walmart, you know that hardly a few seconds elapse until one, two, three, or more shoppers file in behind you.

So I say her name and ask if I may pray for her daughter.

She says, "Here? Now?"

I reply, "Yes, if you are comfortable with that."

"Sure," she says delightedly.

I began the prayer with her name and the declaration that the Lord loves her, knows both her name and the number of hair on her head, collects her tears in His bottle, and is fully aware of a mother's concern for her child with a request that His hand would be fully engaged in alleviating the concern of a loving mother by providing a clear bill of health from the attending physician.

And then I heard myself saying, "You see that redheaded lady in the Vision Center? Her name is Cindy, and she is my wife. I would sure like it if you would be kind enough to let her know of the good report that you are going to receive from the physician."

She indicated that she would and then thanked me. I smiled, wished her a blessed day, and departed. That same evening when Cindy arrived home, she handed me a greeting card, which I presumed she had purchased. I thanked her for the card because she had given me cards on many an occasion, but she said this one was not from her.

My eyes watered as they traced the heartfelt words of gratitude from this loving mother concerning the excellent report that the physician had given. Folks, there are hundreds of such circumstances that are occurring within my "Jerusalem, Judea, and Samaria" every single day, if only, I have eyes to see, ears to hear, and hands and feet to serve.

We must remember that people do not "give a hoot" (South Texan for "they haven't the slightest interest") about what we know until they first know that we care...about them. It matters not one iota that we have three doctorates, four master degrees, five bachelors of arts, or an IQ of 292. They want to know that we are genuinely concerned about their current station in life.

And, oh yes, you need to know that not even one person entered that checkout lane during this entire event. Go figure. It just confirms that He cares enough to handle every necessary detail when we choose to buy into His assignment. I just love (agape) my elder brother (Jesus of Nazareth).

So is He able to bring life into any kind of situation, even those that can approach despair, you know, like a funeral? Well, Jesus declared in John 6:63b, "The words I speak to you are spirit, and they are life", which seems to carry the assurance that sharing His life-giving words can change every type of circumstance from its present scenario to a joyful conclusion. It seems to me that this sort of an uplifting result could be described as having power over existing circumstances.

A recent graduation to glory produced just such a result. One of the adult children of the graduate was in obvious distress and suffering major grief from this loss of her mother. It had resulted from a very recent harsh disagreement with her mother in addition to other ongoing and unresolved conflicts, including a perceived offense caused by a different individual. There was a clearly perceptible tension (darting eyes) and sense of considerable concern exhibited by the majority of the attendees, both young and adult.

Several minutes before the interment service began, it became increasingly obvious that this daughter was in a state of uncontrollable regret and great fear accompanied by the stark realization that any chance of reconciliation with her mother lay before her in the casket. Her arms jerked out of control. She shouted the name of her sister as though she felt her sibling might somehow help her in her now desperate dilemma. The intensity of her nightmare manifested as, while at the casket's edge, she began to lift her leg as though she wanted to get into the casket with her mother. It was such a heart-rending scene. Could anything reverse such a circumstance?

As the minister prepared to commence, he turned to the guitarist and requested a chorus, which soothingly reminds us that, when Jesus arrives on the scene, the power of the evil one is broken. Additionally His presence can dry the tears of pain, and further how He can take any amount of gloom and replace it with His glory.

As these words permeated the air, a discernible peace began to settle over the scene. No one had to tell you that this was happening. You were inarguably able to visibly observe this transformation, and by the completion of the third repetition of that chorus, there were no jerking hands and no desperate shouts of hopelessness. No, indeed, a calm was fully settling in, a hush that can only be delivered by the Prince of Peace (Isa. 9:6). And at the subsequent gathering with friends and family, there was a visible change of attitude toward those perceived to have previously brought offense— smiles, touching of hands, and free-flowing conversation.

Friends, it is extremely difficult under the best of circumstances to reverse the effects of offenses, but when the increased pressure and stress of the loss of a family member is added in, nothing less than the direct intervention of heaven can deliver the power to overcome the circumstances of this dimension. So what about you? Do you have a personal relationship with this Great King? If so, what is the quality of your friendship? Are you on speaking terms with Him? How frequently do you "call Him up" (Jer. 33:3) and just settle in for a quiet time of refreshing and an upgrading in your understanding? Can you think of a more wonderful time than this very moment?

You can rest assured that, just as He showed up in these extremely difficult conditions, this extravagant lover (1 John 3:1-4:16) can be counted upon to deliver exactly what you need most in your immediate circumstances. He loves it so very much when we answer His knock at our door (Rev. 3:20). In fact, He will come in and sup. I am certain that such an event can only be described as leisurely, magnificent, and luxurious with absolutely no regard for expense. What a joy-filled event!

Would you care to participate? What is there that you could do at this very moment that could possibly be more rewarding than this, to be in the indescribable presence of the righteous King of Glory? He responds to personal invitation. You can be certain of that. I know from personal experience. Yes, even me.

On some occasions, the Holy Spirit obviously directs us into providing one-on-one ministry to those nearby. But it is also a certainty that we should also be intentionally alert to those situations that are occurring all around us and, having become aware of them, to ask Holy Spirit for heavenly input as to how we can be of service on an ongoing basis.

Recently my wife and I took her mother for a midday meal in a wonderful home-cooking restaurant in Houston. One of the fun things there is that they toss fresh, hot rolls to you. In fact they are known as "home of the throw'd roll." As the goings-on occurred, my attention was drawn to a lady sitting alone at a nearby table. I looked at her briefly on three occasions, observed her demeanor, and discerned she was sorting through some challenges.

After mentioning this to Mom and Cindy, I decided to approach the lady with the encouraging words, "The Lord wants you to know that He loves you. He knows the number of hair on your head, and He places your tears in His bottle."

I then presented her with a "Trust me" card. At which point, she softly responded with a sincere "thank you" and continued with the comment that she was sorting through multiple issues in her life.

I returned to our table, and some fifteen minutes later, she finished her meal and walked to our table, addressed the three of us, and declared how appreciative she was of the caring concern that had been shown her. Discerning that she would be receptive, I asked if she would allow us to pray a prayer of agreement with her, and she smiled and agreed. I prayed softly with my eyes open. I so enjoy observing the work of the Holy Spirit as He manifests change in circumstances and countenances. We completed the prayer with moist eyes. She genuinely thanked us and departed with a changed countenance.

There are several definitions as to what revival is, but events such as this certainly seem to fit the criteria of the definition of revivify, "a bringing back to life." And Holy Spirit is now upgrading my recognition that such opportunity can daily be found nearby wherever I may be. Lord, my ongoing prayer is that You will please continue to increase my awareness, sensitivity, and willingness to make myself available to perform this crucial ministry of compassion for the multitude. It is so very essential and wonderfully revitalizing.

This is the desired extravagant result mentioned in the opening sentences of chapter one of this very document. Such results are exhilarating for both the recipient and the giver. Try it, You will like it.

In the recruiting period of His ministry, Jesus declared that fishing for men would become a priority in the lives of His new students. It also becomes obvious to each of His followers that He used language familiar to all within His hearing so that any person with ears to hear could, if they were genuinely seeking truth, quickly grasp his meaning. I have come to wonder whether we utilize that technique to its fullest effect. When noticing all the many hundreds of fishing lures available in stores and, further, when looking into the tackle boxes of those dedicated fishing persons, it is immediately apparent that the "one size fits all" approach is doomed to failure. There are numerous sizes, there are many colors, there are various materials used, there are top-water lures, and then others are set at varying depths beneath the surface of the water. There is also the matter of weather conditions, and not to be disregarded is the necessity of going to where they are on any given day. They may be located just a few feet from where we have been so diligently seeking. This is so wonderfully demonstrated by the Lord in the all-night fishing episode of Peter, James, John, and friends, as recorded in Luke 5:1-11 and John 21:1-11.

It is so clear that there is more than one method needed to assure the catch available on any particular day. We must constantly be aware that our favorite evangelistic lure may have worked wonderfully yesterday. It might work well again in the future, but today it must be placed back in the tackle box and replaced by a completely different one.

Please consider the following as examples: if the person before me is carrying an offense against a parent, pastor, priest, rabbi, the president of the United States, or some other person, a "come to Jesus" plea will likely be ineffective until the grievances have been suitably addressed and a releasing of offense has occurred. In a different encounter where the person has no church history whatsoever, in fact, the only thing they may know about Jesus is how to spell His name, if that. A significantly different lure is likely to be needed. A third and different scenario can be a physical impairment or injury that is so painful and impedes or prevents the ability or desire to have dialogue about any matter other than the cessation of those debilitating circumstances.

So is there a single method that can bridge these three vignettes and all the countless other variations that we may encounter? Just as before, attaching to Jesus's example is always the correct path since He only did and said what He heard from His Father. When asked about the great commandment (Matt. 22:35–40), He made it abundantly clear that our unrestrained love for God and our neighbor (those nearby) was clearly to be the centerpiece of our lifestyle (our daily conduct; behavior).

He both demonstrated and stated on various occasions that He had heart-driven compassion on the multitude and individuals, which denotes suffering with them, to include empathy, mercy, and tender affection. It thus appears certain that my personal evangelization should proceed out of a caring, tenderhearted affection and mercy toward all those who are nearby. I have given considerable study, prayer, and thought to formulating a workable definition for the word "love." I understand that many fellow humans have approached this as well. I have come to the decision that, as always, it is essential to look to the expert when approaching such a monumental task. When asked which was the greatest commandment of all, Jesus clearly stated that we must love the Lord our God with all our heart, soul, mind, and strength and He then continued with the declaration that the second is like the first. That is, we must love our neighbor as we love ourselves.

Hold it right there. It is quite clear from that statement that we are to love ourselves, is it not? And obviously we are to love our neighbor in exactly the same manner as we love ourselves, correct? Can there be any doubt that God accurately estimated and adequately supplied every conceivable need of all of mankind (Rev. 13:8b) even before the creation of Adam on the sixth day? That would clearly seem to include both my neighbor and me, so I am proposing that an accurate definition for love is accurately estimating and adequately supplying the needs of any human being that Abba Father chooses to place in my path. It seems that this can best occur by developing an approach that clearly demonstrates that I genuinely care about them, all of their basic needs, all of their disappointments, their physical maladies, and their soul state, in short, every concern I have for myself.

I must realize that this is an approach that takes both considerable time and determined effort if I am to achieve the desired fruitful results. Trite comments such as "This too shall pass" or "It's always darkest just before dawn" are often perceived, and correctly it seems to me, as an attempt to stop further discussion rather than expressions of heart-driven concern.

In short, it takes work. Much, hard work. It requires that I passionately evaluate what I would like others to do for me if circumstances were reversed. This renewing of my mind most assuredly will not occur with microwave speed, but must be understood to be a low-heat, slow-cooking event. And just like those so incredibly wonderful barbecued pork ribs, it is so worth the time and effort. Watching the dim light in their eyes change to a warm glow and hearing those lifeless words transition into expressions of attainable hope brings an indescribable exultation to the hearts of both the recipient and the giver. It is oh so rewarding to observe the dunamis enabled metamorphosis that has occurred right before your eyes.

It has very recently become obvious to me that this type of revival is what Jesus was feasting on when He declared to His disciples that He had meat to eat of which they were not aware. It seems certain to me that it matters not how many such testimonies you have heard nor how many books you may have read describing such, until you have a personal history laden with these joy-filled moments, you are unable to grasp the impact of overarching joy that accompanies such transfigurations. My sincere prayer is that, if you are not yet personally familiar with such an event you will determine in your heart today, this very day, to ask the Lord to place such an opportunity in your path and to enable you through the guidance of the Holy Spirit to experience such lavish joy. The Lord will never set you up for failure, that is, He will never leave you nor forsake you. And you can be certain of this, you need have no concern about the results because it's not about your reputation. He accomplishes such extravagant results for His name's sake, and once you have had the experience of just one such event, you may be certain that you will then begin to seek other such events. It might even be seen as addictive. Well, perhaps not addictive, but certainly most desirable.

The end-time harvest is fully observable, so absolutely essential and unquestionably attainable. Having said that surely requires that we evaluate the present state in which the believing church (John 14:6) finds herself. Can we truthfully declare that today's church-at-large is presently at a level that we find written of the church in Acts 2 and beyond? Can we further verify that the church general has arrived at the level promised by our Lord Jesus Christ when He stated that the works He did would be done and greater works than those because He would go to the Father? And are we, the believing church, all aligned under the unity banner prescribed by our Lord in His priestly prayer as recorded in John chapter seventeen?

If we discover that the body of believers that comprises the church-at-large is deficient in any of those three areas, it seems clear that there is yet much to be done. It is absolutely certain that the vehicle of prayer is what is necessary to remove any roadblock that stands in the path of fulfillment of the Great Commission.

So what things are we personally to be doing? Each of us knows that we individually are daily to be about the Master's business of having compassion on the multitude. That, as previously stated, means beginning with those who are nearby. But what else might we do to enlarge or broaden the assault on the kingdom of darkness? We know that sending missionaries both here at home in the United States and around the world has historically been and still is, very effective.

A more recent and most wonderful approach is to harvest the secular universities, colleges, and other such educational establishments as sources of supply to provide, prepare, and send thousands of young men and women into the seven most influential divisions of any society anywhere in our world. These seven divisions have come to be identified as: arts (to include entertainment and sports), business, communication (includes the media), deity (religion or church), education, family, and government.

America has long been a magnet to the nations of the world and viewed as a desirable place to receive higher education. When we consider that these institutions of higher learning with their greater diversity of education can become the foundation upon which nations can be crafted, it becomes immediately obvious that this can become a treasure trove of opportunity to disciple nations and evangelize our planet.

If we assimilate these young minds as freshmen and lead them through a Romans 12:2 transformation over a period of four or more years, it is not difficult to see that a major global shift can be achieved. And if each of these students will seek out, disciple, and mentor as few as five new adherents, it will be quite shocking to see the results that can occur, when replicated, over a ten-year period. And just imagine what can occur in other nations when one of their own returns home and displays a lifestyle as well and proceeds to share their newfound relationship with the King of the Universe.

Imagine the many differences that will occur when untold thousands of college students begin to superimpose a relational theology (Ps.16:11, 46:10; Phil. 3:10; James 4:8) on whatever field of academic endeavor they choose to pursue. And this improvement will occur in far less time than we suppose because the Holy Spirit who leads us into all truth will soon begin to supply solutions to a diversity of world-class challenges that were previously considered to be insoluble.

One such campus organization with a history reaching back to 1947 is known as Chi Alpha (XA) Christian Fellowship and can be located on many secular campuses throughout America and in many nations of the world.

But you say, "I'm well past college age. What can I do?"

Enable (provide money) your child, grandchild, niece or nephew, or young neighbor to locate an institution that offers such an outreach. And if you are unable to enable, at a minimum, recommend he or she attend such a one. Then cover his or her decision with a mountain of prayer.

But you say, "What about folks in America or foreign countries that simply cannot afford college and may struggle just to support their family. How can they receive a "Master's" degree (Acts 4:13) in relational theology?"

Well, they surely need a Bible-teaching home church, a small group is essential to address the difficulties of daily living and a Bible. And should they be unable to afford one, The Gideons International (TGI@GIDEONS.ORG) now operates in more than 180 nations of the world and offers free Bibles in many languages. And most certainly, a prayer life is an absolute must from the beginning and is essential to continue daily (Acts 17:26–28) until life's end.

But they can also access a vast amount of teaching, preaching, and mentoring that is available to them, often 24-7, which is terrific for shift workers, retirees, and the home-bound folk, much of it without cost on internationally broadcast television and radio to include shortwave broadcasting and of course, the Internet as well. It is globally widespread.

But you say, "I'm a shut-in on limited income. What can I do to help?"

First and foremost, prayer is the most powerful tool on the planet. Just how important is it? 1 Samuel 12:23 reminds us that it is a sin to fail to pray. But where do you begin? Start with 2 Peter 3:9 (God's heart) and 1 Timothy 2:1-2 to bring peace and quiet into your life. Most certainly, pray for the peace of Jerusalem (Ps.122:6), the city that is the hub of our world. Then just have a normal conversation with the Lord Jesus (the Prince of Peace)(Isa.9:6) as though He were your very best friend, because that is exactly who He wants to be for you.

Please know this. The way you learn to pray is by praying. It is not more complicated than that. Just be sincere and listen for a still, small voice that is comforting, relaxing, filled with peace, and so very encouraging. You will then experience a lovely, indescribable, joy-filled presence, and as it begins to settle over you, simply ask the Lord for the direction He wants you to pray. You may sense that you are to pray for a specific coworker, a neighbor, family member, or person that you had not thought about in quite a long time. Then ask the Lord to extend His favor over this person and draw him or her closer to Himself and to be for him or her whatever it is that he or she most needs at that very moment.

Don't be surprised if you soon hear from those people that you just prayed for. It frequently happens that way. The most important step is to begin today. Please consider the following eye-opener by Dr. Peter Kreeft, author and professor of philosophy at Boston College (copied from *Guidepost*),

> "I strongly suspect that if we saw all the difference even the tiniest of our prayers make, and all the people these prayers were destined

to affect, and all the consequences of those prayers down through all the centuries, we would be so paralyzed with awe at the power of prayer, that we would be unable to get up off our knees for the rest of our lives."

Oh my! Did that impact you to the depths of your being? That is such power-filled truth, and it appears obvious that every one of us has a crucial part to play in the gathering of the final harvest. The great question seems to be what action that will each of us-yes, both you and I-determine to take. And how soon will we begin to educate ourselves as just listed above?

I've read through the Bible more than twenty-eight times, and I find no place where the twelve apostles went to the University of Jerusalem or any such institute of higher learning. I do, however, find in Acts 4:5-13 that the Sanhedrin marveled at the activity and message of Peter and perceived that, while Peter and John were clearly uneducated and untrained men, the Sanhedrin recognized they had been with Jesus. That becomes particularly enlightening when you consider that this Sanhedrin was the very same group of leaders who had failed to recognize that Jesus was indeed the very Son of God. And the apostle Paul, formerly Saul of Tarsus, made the clear comment that, while he was educated (a second-generation Pharisee) and had been under Gamaliel's teaching (at his knee), his ability and understanding came through a direct revelation from Jesus and was not as a result of man's teaching (Acts 20:24-25; Gal. 1:11-12), not even the apostles.

And during his Damascus Road experience, Saul (soon to be renamed Paul), asks a question that clearly reveals that, even with all of his education, he is posing a most revealing and shocking query, "Who are you, Lord?"

Just like the Sanhedrin, he knew about the Lord, but he did not know the Lord. I am absolutely not degrading the value of education. However, education alone without an ongoing, personal, intimate relationship with heaven through the person of the Holy Spirit (to include soaking/abiding in His presence)(Ps. 16:11) is simply not going to bring about results that exceed those accomplished by the Lord Jesus Christ during his three-and-a-half-year ministry on this planet. While it is absolutely essential to know the Word of God, it is even more crucial to know the God of the Word (Phil. 3:10, "That I may KNOW Him").

Jesus confirms this in John 5:39-40 when He informs the Pharisees that they faithfully read the law, for, in those words, they thought they had eternal life. He was, of course, fully aware that they had memorized all of it. Yet they would not come to Him, the Word incarnate. We must never forget that in John 5:19, 30, Jesus stated that He, the Son of God in whom the Father was well pleased, could of Himself do nothing without the Father's direction. I dare not be so arrogant as to think that I could do greater works than Jesus did with any less heavenly input than Jesus had. Agreed? At our present time in history, the church typically gathers around a message, while the children of Israel chose to gather around His presence. Wisdom dictates that it is advisable that I not even entertain such an insultingly disrespectful and, may I say, an even prideful thought that I could do any less.

I have been blessed to know three men of God who are true bishops. Each of them has planted or begun fifteen or more churches throughout various nations of the world, including Guatemala, Honduras, Jamaica, Mexico, Peru, and the United States of America. If starting, staffing, and, in a great percentage of cases initially, pastoring many of these facilities were not enough, there is the constant attention required to enable the ongoing daily work required by each of them. Additionally, there are the repairs, which are a continuing necessity, and, of course, the enlarging of each of the facilities to accommodate the resultant growth brought about by the harvest. Add to that the selecting, teaching, mentoring, maturing, and undergirding that is so very necessary to develop pastors and staff who, of necessity, must eventually become self-sustaining and fully capable of providing the day-to-day demands of the facility for which they have been entrusted with responsibility. The prime determining factor as to the period of time required to achieve self-sufficiency is the spiritual maturity level at which the pastor and any staff, whether volunteer or paid, have attained.

Nothing that has been said thus far comes as a surprise to any who have effected a church plant, that is, the ground zero beginning of a new work. What may be different is our mind-set of such a new start. Not every new work necessarily requires the erection of a physical church structure. More than a few such beginnings have occurred especially in remote areas, in existing structures, perhaps a private home or an existing empty structure. They may begin as a care group, small group, Bible study, cell group, or such. While these do not require that a new structure be built, they do necessitate the same attention to the instruction of each leader; a library that may be as simple as a full-study Bible in the appropriate language, perhaps a Strong's Hebrew/ Greek concordance; ideally a Bible handbook; a minister's handbook; and a guide to leading a small group. It is more than obvious that the most essential components to assure success are daily prayer, quiet time, hosting the presence of heaven, and ongoing immersion in the Word.

You may be wondering why this subject has even been breached. How much money would it require to buy a small library for such an undertaking? What else, minimally speaking, is needed to commence such a work in some remote village or area? It requires that an equipped believer with a heart for kingdom ministry and who loves his or her neighbor as much as himself or herself be sent into such areas and that the sent one(s) not be muzzled by a litany of restrictions that hamper the ability to achieve the goal that is set before them. It is extremely difficult to comprehend the manifold difficulties encountered in such undertakings when considering them from a cozy, air-conditioned boardroom with a full stomach, a nice vehicle, and home at your beck and call.

I don't make these observations without some hands-on experience, both in the boardroom setting and on the mission field in the African bush, the Mexican poverty arena, and the Jamaican daily struggle for existence. You may have been in the presence of these unique servants. They come at the invitation of your pastor and pour out their vision from hearts driven by the burning in their bones. They don't whine about the daily difficulties of the ministry. In fact they are likely to discuss the most difficult daily challenges only during the meal that follows at the local restaurant after the church services are concluded.

If you haven't already done so, ask your pastor if you can be a part of that gathering. All that I am asking is that a tender heart be extended toward these lovers of mankind when establishing restrictions as to how mission monies are to be used by these frontline heroes of heaven.

Please understand that I am not personally one of these servants, but I have been with them and can attest to their determined outpouring of aga'pe on an ongoing basis. Jesus surely is pleased with such since they are wholeheartedly charging ahead with His commission to disciple all nations (Matt. 28:19–20). Dare I be any less ecstatic than my Savior and Lord? Hmmm. Please consider this with an openly tender heart and mind. selah

Earlier the question was posed as to whether the believing church-at-large (John 14:6) is delivering the fullness of Jesus's declarations in Matthew 10:7–8 and Mark 16:15–18. It is both absolutely essential and, at the same time, challenging for many leaders to address the entirety of every declaration made in those two passages. Perhaps the greatest roadblock is the willingness of each congregant to openly admit that, first of all, he or she has a spiritual problem that is beyond his or her own ability to resolve, that is, apart from the direct involvement of the Holy Spirit.

Which of us wants to consider the possibility that we are actually the designated target of one or perhaps more evil spirits whose sole purposes are to kill, steal, and destroy us? We need only to read the daily activities of Jesus as recorded in Matthew, Mark, Luke, John, and Acts to recognize that such evil was well known to exist in every level of society, whether rich or poor and regardless of age from birth to the senior years. And we must remember that heaven knows the entire range of history (the former things; the latter things) (Isa. 42:9). Hence Jesus has clearly warned us that evil spirits would continue to be a genuine threat and that they are to be expelled from humans.

Inarguably, evil spirits are a powerful entity (seven sons of Sceva)(Acts 19:11–17). Thus we must understand that there are some preparatory actions that absolutely must be taken before attempting any such expulsion. Few, if any of us, would attempt to reload pistol, rifle, or shotgun shells without first educating ourselves to the potential dangers involved. It is no less necessary to arm ourselves before any attempted expulsion is considered. And as always, we should look to the experts before doing anything.

Jesus is obviously the expert in all spiritual matters. The Bible has much to teach us from both the Old and New Testaments. One anointed human source, Reverend Derek Prince, has done the biblical research and pioneered teaching both on generational curses and demonology/ spiritual warfare. The value of this wisdom, understanding, and practical (hands-on) application cannot be overstated. Avail yourself of any of the fifty books available via www. derekprince.com. Especially *Blessings or Curse* and *They Shall Expel Demons* are particularly recommended as a great place to begin. And please know that total forgiveness for all wrongs (no exceptions) that have been suffered is absolutely essential if the desired results are to be achieved.

It seems safe to declare that almost all of us genuinely delight in receiving gifts, especially when those presents are totally unexpected. What a joy, right? While I have so very many gifts to be thankful for, two such extravagant gifts immediately come to my memory. The first occurred back in 1982 when I was in the throes of unemployment and could have sunk into the depths of sadness, perhaps even that dreadful state of depression. The good news is that I had chosen instead to establish a daily regimen of praise, prayer, thanksgiving, worship, intimacy, and Bible immersion with my three awesome heavenly friends. My family was made aware that these times were not to be interrupted except with bona fide emergencies and fully understood that "Dad, do you know where the Cheerios are?" clearly did not fall within the emergency criteria.

As you may have already experienced, each day requires the ongoing pursuit of the next employment opportunity. On the day that the first extravagant gift came, I was reading my Bible, engaging in thanksgiving, praising, worshipping, and such. I had just consulted my wristwatch to confirm that there was sufficient time before my next scheduled job interview.

Forty-five minutes later, I came to myself and realized that, for the very first time in my life, I was speaking in my heavenly language. Mind you, I had not been seeking that gift; nor had I been reading information on it. Nor was I reading in Acts chapters 1 and 2. Nor had I recently been taught of it. Nor was any human being with me telling me that I needed to seek it.

No doubt, it was a totally unexpected gift. Such a superb gift and one that continues to keep on empowering and emboldening, even to this very day. I have since learned that I can increase my heavenly vocabulary by utilizing it on a daily basis. Yes I am certain that, just as I practiced my earthly language from the early days of my childhood and thus increased that vocabulary, I can grow my heavenly language as well. I know that to be scriptural for when I visit the events listed in the book of Acts, chapter 2 verses 5 through 11, I am told that persons of many different languages heard the heaven-directed language in their native tongue.

And when I recall that I am actually talking directly to God (1 Cor. 14:2), it is so invigorating to understand that He alone can understand this form of communication, definitely a hotline to heaven. It is truly an ever-present help (Eph. 6:18; Jude 20; Rom. 8:26) against those recurring assaults from the accuser of the brethren. To Abba Father, I most joyfully declare my profound gratitude. Amen!

The second superb gift occurred during an early morning awakening that had all the trappings of joy saturating it. I had secured that acoustic guitar from its case and begun to fill the air of my bedroom with a variety of worth-ship (celebrating His worth to me) and joyous exclamation. Think, joy to the world!

I heard myself saying aloud as I strummed, "Lord, my words fall far short of the ability to declare the extent of the love and appreciation I am experiencing at this moment, so you will just have to read my heart."

At this time in my life, I was being so powerfully impacted with the available transformation (*metamorphoo*, Greek) communicated in Romans 12:2, that I had previously jotted down the declaration, "I refuse to be who I used to be."

Well, much to my surprise and delight, from out of my mouth flowed both melody and words to wit, "I refuse to be who I used to be. I'm a child of the Great I Am, and He has given me the mind of Christ. And I can do all things through Him."

And minutes later came part two, "So, I refuse to be who I used to be. The Holy Spirit has become my guide. He is leading me into all of the truth, and Jesus is ever at my side."

Need I tell you of the unrestrained joy that overarched me? And get this cherry topping on the whipped cream! This occurred on the morning of the seventieth anniversary (three score and ten, Ps. 90:10) of my birth date.

Well, time marches on, and I am yet again surprised by the events of the morning of March 5, 2015. I awakened at 5:38 a.m. and felt led to get out ye old acoustic and proceed to send melodic praise skyward to the third heaven.

After a few moments, there was the sense that heaven had a third part for the "I Refuse to Be" chorus. Shortly I began to recite and then repeat and subsequently pen the following: "Please refuse to be who you used to be. Let God's kingdom be your lifetime goal. Your mind cannot conceive the love He has for you, as daily He works to make you whole."

It was another wonderful surprise from my beloved Jehovah Sneaky. I never saw it coming. What a treat! I recall previously reading some very extravagant words, "Delight yourself also in the Lord, and He shall give you the desires of your heart (Ps. 37:4). selah

So what are some of the most recent adventures of the Holy Spirit that this seeker has been permitted to experience? Wait until you hear these four delights.

Cindy and I were the recipients of several of those wonderful restaurant gift cards that are so generously given to staff members during pastoral appreciation month. We keep them with us so we can use them to celebrate special meals, most often with Cindy's mom. Such was the case a few weeks ago. We elected to visit the Cheesecake Factory and were honored to be served by Camilla, a most knowledgeable and fully attentive professional.

As is my practice, I commented to Camilla that we soon would be giving thanks for our meal and wondered if there were anything that we could bring to heaven's attention on her behalf.

With absolutely no hesitation, she related that she had been doing her very best to serve her mother who had health issues and had lived in Nevada until the very day before. Camilla had brought her mother and sister to Texas to live so she could more effectively meet her mom's needs (love spoken here). I commented that long-distance assistance could place a strain on both the budget and the emotions, which she softly confirmed. (Holy Spirit said to tip her generously, I obeyed.) I asked her if I might pray softly for her, her sister, and her mother. She smiled and then, exhibiting unrestrained joy, agreed.

I reminded heaven of her generous and honoring heart, pronounced the favor of heaven upon her, presented her with one of the "Trust me" cards, and smiled. I got a totally unexpected treat. She smiled, stepped very close to me, leaned over, gave me a huge bear hug, and joyfully proclaimed a "thank you so very much."

These are treasured moments that fully enable you to better understand what the Master Teacher (Jesus) meant when he proclaimed that He had meat to eat of which others had absolutely no clue. When we learn that others have far greater needs than we first supposed and further, then allow the Holy Spirit to fill those vacuums (with a small assist from us), all heaven is completely engaged in the performance of the restoration of the most difficult of circumstances and generously restores the hope of the downtrodden. What a joyous turnabout. I truly wish you had been there, but hey, why not follow the prompting of the Holy Spirit in a similar celebration? I'm quite confident there are countless more to be had.

The second event, while also an amazing celebration, is of an entirely different nature. I received a call from a fellow believer who was heavily laden with spiritual assaults from the satanic realm. And further, these intolerable attacks had begun at the age of nine and had continued for several decades with various treacherous assaults including the trauma of Vietnam Service. They had now reached the point where the victim knew it was imperative that they cease, that the deliverance must be complete. The victim had stated that it mattered not how many hours the cleansing required. He would do whatever was necessary.

I assured the candidate that his willingness to do everything that was needed was a necessary ingredient to success. I further advised that he read two books by Reverend Derek Prince, *Blessing or Curse* and *They Shall Expel Demons*. I explained that it was necessary to properly identify, completely prepare, and fully recognize the seriousness of such a bold undertaking. I also felt led of the Holy Spirit to recommend that, after reading the two books by Reverend Prince, he follow the direction in Habakkuk 2:2 and write down what he was willing to do to accomplish the entirety of his expectation and to assure that there would not be a return of any of the current unauthorized occupants, nor any of their associated minions.

I further strongly insisted the absolute necessity that total forgiveness be given to every individual who had ever wronged, abused, brutalized, or emotionally victimized this individual and made it clear that there could not be even one exception. I notified this person that he must sever any and all ties, if any, with the occult, including secret societies, Ouija boards, palm reading, fortune-telling, and horoscopes. He was to cease the worship of all false gods, including Buddha, Allah, and all cults. And he was to confess and renounce all sexual sin including adultery, pornography, incest, homosexuality, and bestiality. This is not meant to be understood as the definitive list. It is rather to be an indicator that every association with any activity outside the Trinity of Jehovah God, the Lord and Savior Jesus the Christ, and the person of the Holy Spirit must be confessed, renounced, and permanently abandoned.

The excellent news is that the results were truly wonderful. There were five expulsions, but you need to understand that this result was achieved only after ten continuous hours of determined prayer. We must understand that these enemies have occupied territory in some instances for more than fifty years, and they do not intend to be evicted without the heavenly authority (*exousia*, Greek) that is solely provided through Jesus's name. And this eviction can occur only after earthly license (permission) is granted by citizens of earth.

This requirement for earthly permission came into effect when God (Gen. 1:26) declared that man would have dominion over things on earth. At that time, God locked Himself out of earthly decisions (He gave us free moral agency) unless and until man invited Him through the vehicle of prayer ("Thy kingdom come, thy will be done, on earth just as it is in heaven").

You very well may wonder why I have chosen to address this event so strongly. When studying the day-by-day activities of the Lord Jesus, it becomes so apparent that He addressed the needs of the people before He taught them. He fed them when needed, healed them, and delivered them. Have you ever wondered why churches today reverse the sequence of these events? That is assuming, of course, that these required needs are even addressed.

It seems quite noteworthy that, when shopping for a vehicle, one thing most consumers are interested in is whether the vehicle under consideration has sufficient power to meet a variety of needs, and yet on many occasions at this time in church history, few demonstrations of power are even discussed, let alone provided. It appears that we are far more likely to pass the offering plate with the expectation that the congregants will willingly give, than we are likely to be offering them solutions to their great needs. Have we forgotten the words of Jesus as recorded in John 14:12, "Most assuredly, I say to you, he who believes in me, the works that I do he will do also; and greater than these he will do, because I go to My Father"? John 14:13 heightens this declaration with, "And whatever you ask in my name, that I will do, that the Father may be glorified in the Son." And if that were not enough, John 14:14 drives the final nail with this potent promise, "If you ask anything in my name, I will do it."

Do we believe the Son of God tells the truth? Do we believe the written Word that proclaims, "Jesus Christ is the same yesterday, today and forever"? Do we truly believe that Jesus is still alive today and able to perform His promises? If we actually believe the promises of the Son of God who only did/ said what He saw and heard from the Father and who is the same yesterday, today, and forever, why on earth (as it is in heaven) would we fail to provide to all humanity everything that Jesus demonstrated on a daily basis?

Consider this, please. If there is no sickness, affliction, or spiritual torment in heaven and Jesus instructed us to pray to the Father, "Thy kingdom come, thy will be done on earth as it is in heaven," it seems clear enough that whatever is not allowed in heaven must not be permitted on earth. In short, if it is not intended, it must not be permitted. Profoundly declare,"No, we kingdom kids are not having that"! That is a truth of living life in the spirit. With this crucial understanding, every sincere Spirit-guided servant in the kingdom of God must choose to be daily declaring the availability of the entire bounty of heaven to every member of mankind with which we are privileged to make contact. What follows is clearly the only way to become a friend of the one who is the only way to the Father. "You are my friends if you do whatever I command you" (John 15:14). My desire is to achieve that distinction. Are you on board for that?

The third thrilling recent event occurred as a result of a concern expressed by a coworker where Cindy enables others to see their best. (Cindy is an optician.) Her coworker shared that her dad was in the ICU of a hospital in San Antonio with a tumor further complicated by internal bleeding. I asked whether the family would consider prayer. Cindy asked and was told yes. Further I was told that I should go after 1:00 p.m. due to other surgery preparations. I arrived at 2:30 and proceeding to the patient's room, found it unoccupied. The nursing station advised me that the coworker's father was prepped and made ready for surgery, which was expected to last for three and a half hours. I was directed to the waiting area, where I shortly located five family members.

I asked whether we might form a prayer circle, to which they agreed. I told them that I always asked heaven to provide THE physician who was best for the conditions under which the patient labored and that there be other Christ followers in the operating room as well. We agreed in prayer, and after only one hour and fifteen minutes, the surgeon arrived to report the results and prognosis. He stated that he had not performed what was originally planned, but he had first removed the tumor and then cauterized the source of the internal bleeding. When asked for his opinion as to future rehab, he stated that he would have the patient walking around the next day. He then made the shocking statement that he didn't understand why he was chosen to perform the operation, as his expertise was with kidney surgery. The wife looked at me, and we simultaneously commented that we knew exactly why he was chosen. Folks, God cares enough to provide His very best!

The fourth delightful event occurred even more recently, on Thursday, March 12, 2015. I chose to record the date to affirm that Jesus Christ is absolutely the same, yesterday, today, and forever. My phone rang at 8:15 a.m., and Hector advised me that his wife's fifteen-year-old niece was in the emergency room with a ruptured appendix and that they were awaiting a surgeon to perform the crucial operation.

As is my custom, I prayed in agreement with Hector and his wife Elva that God would once again provide THE surgeon of His choice and there would be believers in the operating room. In a subsequent conversation with Hector, he told me that the necessary surgery was not performed until just before 1:00 p.m. Understandably the family was more than slightly concerned with the delay, that is, until they learned the expertise of the attending surgeon was specifically in the arena of ruptured appendix. It was subsequently learned that the surgeon had been attending to previously scheduled surgeries, hence the delay.

I continue to be overwhelmed with the magnitude of the love demonstrated by this God who is love and will continue to proclaim His astounding love forever. There can be no doubt. This is assuredly the lover you have been so desperately seeking. His promise is Call unto me and I will answer" (Jer. 33:3). His line is never busy. You never get put on hold. There's never a long distance charge. Call now and frequently. And expect His very best!

So I was at the funeral home honoring the graduation (home-going) of my father-in-law. I went into the refreshment room, grabbed a bottle of water, took a seat, and was soon approached by the guest/friend of one of the grandchildren, a young man perhaps thirty years of age.

He pulled up a chair, looked me straight in the eyes, and declared, "I don't believe the Bible. I think a bunch of well-meaning old guys just wrote some words of guidance and encouragement for people to follow."

I thought, "Okay, I've still got Jesus to tell him about."

He promptly continued with, "And I don't think I believe in Jesus either."

Internally, I was remembering that, in Matthew 10:16–20, Jesus declared that, in the last days, we would be brought before authorities and asked for a testimony and that we should not consider beforehand what we should say because, in that hour, the Holy Spirit would give us the needed words.

So internally, I was thinking and praying, "All right, Holy Spirit, I need those words now."

I heard these words inside me, "So, do you believe that Julius Caesar really lived and walked this planet?"

He affirmed that he did. I asked him why he chose to believe that, and he followed with the idea that history recorded it. I knew that initially using the Bible as my historical source would not be wise since he had already proclaimed that he didn't trust it. I asked him whether he had heard of Flavius Josephus, and he said he had not. I continued with the fact that he was a trusted and widely known historian and that, as well, he was not a follower of Jesus the Christ. But he had fully substantiated the signs, wonders, and miracles attributed to Jesus in the Bible. I further told him that there were in fact more writings about Jesus and they were written more closely after His death (and therefore more likely to be accurate) than those of Pliny the Younger and Herodotus, whose pertinent historical documents are accepted (assumed) to be fact. Only seven copies extant support the existence of Pliny the Younger; only eight extant copies support the existence of Herodotus. Yet there are five thousand Greek copies (with 99 percent accuracy) of the New Testament, supporting the existence, life, and activities of Jesus Christ.

But get this. I was soon to learn the actual reasons for his disbelief. I asked this man what his growing-up years had been like. He indicated that a senior family member had pitted all thirty-nine adult family members against each other. Not even one of them interacted with any of the others.

Just then we were told that the memorial service was shortly to commence.

The proceedings were indeed a celebration as many friends, coworkers, acquaintances, and family members lauded, applauded, and commended the celebrant. At the end, I motioned for this young man to join me where I was seated. I asked him how he felt about the goings-on.

With absolutely no hesitation, he stated that he felt that he now could and did believe in Jesus. Shocked-actually flabbergasted is more accurate-I asked if he would mind explaining. He continued with the explanation that this was the very first time in his entire life he had ever experienced love being so openly and profusely demonstrated. He added that finally he could actually believe the statements that Jesus was a love gift from God. Further it was now conceivable to him that humans could actually extend love to others in an observable and meaningful way. Think of greatest commandment number two, "Love your neighbor as yourself."

In that moment, I became absolutely certain that the person who learned the most that day was me. It became so obvious to me that, as a truth-bearer, I must totally respect the rights of nonbelievers to frankly and without any interruption or display of so-called "righteous indignation" on my part, allow them to declare their present state of understanding. It is their right to choose whether or not they believe without judging or castigating them with religious diatribes. God has gifted each human with free moral agency (means THEY choose what they will believe), and perhaps the greatest error comes when we charge forward with an attitude, whether spoken or not, that communicates that they are now approaching a state of damnation. Instead we must demonstrate patient listening habits driven by sincere compassion, all the while allowing them to freely verbalize as well as put forth their questions, if any, without interruption.

I am now more than ever convinced that they will be more prone to openly discuss their current objections when they see that we absolutely care about them. Remember, they do not care what we know until they know that we truly do care... about them.

Of this one thing we can be sure. When believers in the Christ witness, we can be certain that we most assuredly are going to be faced with persons who simply are not ready to accept the truth. Their mind is made up. This certainty brings us to consider how we can enable such persons to be willing to take a fresh look at the possibility that they just might be wrong in the way they think.

Let's consider some possible thought-provoking concepts. One that has proven successful is using a radio signal. You ask if they can use their five senses to locate an FM signal. Can you smell a radio signal? Can you touch/feel a radio signal? Can you see a radio signal? Can you hear a radio signal? Can you taste a radio signal? Then lovingly ask why they bother to turn on the radio.

Next, suggest they are able to locate the signal because they have a properly tuned receiver. Another thought-provoker can be concerning an unknown treasure hidden in their backyard. You tell them that a friend with exceptional expertise has used a very powerful metal detector and has learned that a very valuable treasure is available to him. And further, it is actually located very near to him, and all he needs to do is expend the effort to locate this wonderful gift. He then has the option to choose to seek it out, or he can choose to say that he does not believe that it is there or that wonderful things like that never happen to him.

Then you might ask them nicely, "If you don't bother to consider it, how will you know whether you in fact missed out on some tremendous surprise?"

Then there is the individual who says that he or she doesn't believe that Jesus is the only way to God the Father. He or she continues with the comment that he or she feels Hinduism has some good concepts and that Islam has some helpful ideas. And of course, there are the philosophical teachings of Aristotle, Plato, Socrates, and others.

With gentleness and a sincere smile, ask this person which of all of those just mentioned is historically recorded as having overcome death. Then tenderly ask which one of all these has the greatest power? Ask lovingly if he or she would rather call out for help from someone who is still alive or someone who is not. Do not speak this with any arrogance or pride, including spiritual pride. We are talking about a soul that is teetering on the balance between relationship with the only true and living God or eternal separation from Him.

Do not get in a hurry. Don't look at your wristwatch to see what time it is, and for heaven's sake, don't let your mind wander. And just as important, if at any point in the conversation this person chooses to "slam the door," employ wisdom, smile, suggest that perhaps you might get together for further discussion in the near future, ask if you may pray, and then leave this matter in the capable hands of the Holy Spirit. He gets more done in a few seconds than we can in a lifetime because He knows which uncertainty to confront. He is God, and He can read the mind and heart. We aren't, and we can't.

We must recall that God created hell for the devil (satan) and the fallen angels, not for mankind. This is serious business with everlasting implications. 2 Peter 3:9 is a powerful reminder that God is not willing that any perish. I'm reverently certain that He meant any.

Recently I was invited to speak to the body of Christ and, as is my custom, asked the Holy Spirit for direction. I heard quite clearly within me the admonition, "Don't offer them information; offer them transformation."

While delighted, I also desired further guidance. Soon the words began to form in my heart, and "A Tale of Two

Davids" began to evolve. David number one came to be the NBA stalwart David Robinson of the San Antonio Spurs. He had consistently studied and memorized the playbook that his coach Greg Popovich had designed. Coach "Pop" then taught David how to develop the plays. It was, however, up to David to put feet to the plays.

Another David, a shepherd boy who later was to be king of Israel, absorbed Jehovah's audio playbook very diligently. Coach Jehovah told young David how to develop the plays, but as with the first David, young David had to put feet to the plays.

When there was no crowd watching, David Robinson was spending untold hours practicing each of those hundreds of plays over and over again until they became muscle memory. And remember, no crowd was watching. Our shepherd youth doubtless spent countless hours practicing with his slingshot and killed both a bear and a lion, and no crowd was watching. When no one was watching, David Robinson doubtless missed many shot attempts.

Undoubtedly David the shepherd boy missed his mark with his slingshot many hundreds of times when no one was watching. But when the day of tremendous challenge came, both Davids were fully prepared for the main event. David Robinson led his team to a national championship, while David the young shepherd led Israel to a glorious victory over a numerically superior force by defeating their champion, a giant more than nine feet tall.

But the Spirit continued, "Do not miss this fact. Both Davids had spent untold hours of preparation when no one was watching. They both were well practiced and fully prepared when the enormous challenge presented itself."

In our spiritual walk, those hours where there are no spectators has been referred to as "the secret place" or as "quiet time." So is there a playbook for you and me to study, memorize, and put feet to? Of course there is. God's playbook is the library of sixty-six books known to us as the Bible. Well then, is there a coach to demonstrate for us how the plays are to be developed? Can there possibly be a better candidate than the one of whom it was said, "This is my beloved son, in whom I am well pleased; hear ye him" (Matt. 17:5)?

So let's consider Jesus's comment in John 5:19, 30. Please notice that His ongoing procedure is to only do and say what he sees the Father doing and what He hears the father saying. How about John 8:28 and also 12:49–50. Oh, then there is the event recorded in the garden of Gethsemane (Matt. 26:36, 39, 42, 44). Notice that Jesus prayed privately when no one was watching.

You might be thinking, "Sure, but we aren't Jesus"

True, but look at Moses in Exodus 19:3 and following, especially verse 20. Then notice Exodus Chapters 3:3–4; 34:3, 11, 14–16. Each of these events happened when no one else was watching. How about the woman at the well (John 4:5–8); Nicodemus at night (John 3:1–21); and Mary, the sister of Lazarus (Luke 10:38)?

And you might be thinking, "Well, that was then. What about now?"

Excellent observation! Just look at Revelation 3:20, "Behold I stand (present tense) at the door and knock, if any man (singular) will open the door, I will come in and sup (feast) with him (singular)."

Really, c'mon now. Could this be any clearer? The Creator of the Cosmos desires alone time with you. Let's just take this to a human level. Consider for a moment your very best friend. Did you only read about him or her in a book? Did you become best friends simply because someone else just told you about him or her? Or did you become best friends primarily when the two of you were alone, when no crowd was there?

And finally consider this. In whose image and likeness are you made (Gen. 1:26–28)? Isn't it obvious that your creator would make friends in the same manner as you do (one-on-one)? So if He doesn't seem as close as you would like Him to be, what are you both willing and determined to do in order to achieve such a friendship? He is clearly willing and inarguably waiting. And as is so frequently stated in basketball jargon, "The ball is in your court." James 4:8a is a potent reminder, "Draw near to God and he will draw near to you."

Perhaps one of the finest statements ever made concerning the value of such a relationship is recorded by Albert Hibbert, friend and confidant of the world-renowned twentieth-century minister Smith Wigglesworth as he sat fellowshipping at the table in the home of the eighty-six-year-old Smith one week before his death.

Mr. Hibbert recorded the event as follows, Looking at me with tears in his eyes, he said, 'When are you going to move into a realm that YOU (caps mine) have not yet touched and get going for God?'" Touché! Ouch! Just ponder that thought-provoking challenge for a while.

Most recently I have been made aware of an extremely important understanding of the word "testify" or "to witness." My previous best understanding was that it was a verbal declaration of an eyewitness viewing of an event, a presentation of evidence, if you will. But I was so wonderfully overcome to learn the Hebraic understanding of this amazingly revelatory word (Strong's H5749). It has far greater implication than I had previously understood. Notice that it is to duplicate or repeat; to restore (as a sort of reduplication); or witness.

Consider this. When interceding for the healing or restoration of any individual or, for that matter, any situation requiring the miraculous intervention of our Almighty God, would it not be entirely appropriate to "testify" or "witness" of a previous, specific event at which an exact demonstration of the omnipotent power of God had prevailed, and expecting that He now would presently reduplicate the same fullness in the current situation, as He had in the previous exact same set of circumstances? It seems clear that an excellent approach to this would be for recipients of miraculous intervention to be encouraged to publicly declare, witness, or, yes, testify of the specific event(s) that God had previously performed on their behalf.

It further becomes obvious that a major increase in the faith level of those within the hearing of such events would then be encouraged to consider that this awesome God is consistently available to do it again. It seems clear that God's own declaration of His anger when Israel soon forgot His works is justification for initiation of this practice (Ps. 78:11, 106:13).

Shouldn't we commence this immediately and make it an ongoing practice? Compassion for the multitude (Mark 8:2) would seem to be the most compelling reason for such a decision.

Just in case you are wondering, passion is the driving force that brought me to compile this offering. I have no interest in becoming famous. I do not write to impress readers; rather I write to introduce sincere seekers to my elder brother, one Jesus of Nazareth, lately of heaven, so they may learn to appropriate every enabling gift available to each of them and thereby access His promise to do greater works than He did so the multitude may be served Christlike compassion.

I do not desire to be wealthy by world standards. As a matter of fact, Cindy and I are in agreement that we wish to:

- continue to support the drilling of water wells to provide clean drinking water to those who have none;
- provide airfare to the diaspora of Israel to enable them to return to their homeland;
- support missionaries at home and abroad;

- enable the incredible effectiveness of those who choose to live dead among the 6,500 or so unreached people groups that are spiritually dead; and
- continue to increasingly support Christian ministry that harvests secular universities for visionaries who have the wisdom to discern that our planet is in dire need of impassioned servants of the Great King and are determined to demonstrate through their daily lifestyle and further to spiritually replicate themselves wherever they are called to servanthood, whether in these United States or any other nation of the world.

My heart prayer is that you too will become so tired of the current status quo of our present age that you will determine to refuse to be who you used to be and decide instead to fulfill the destiny that you were created to achieve and intentionally begin to mentor at least one person to rise well above what he or she had previously thought was his or her absolute ceiling.

Such effort is very capable of turning our globe into a realm heretofore thought impossible. It takes the cooperation of just three generous and loving entities; heaven, you, and me. Care to give it a whirl? The driving force is aga'pe love. It's the God kind of love that can be understood as there is nothing you can do to make Him love you more. There is nothing you can do to make Him love you less. He owns everything and wants to give it to you in unfathomable abundance (John10:10b) as a free gift available to you through an intimate, ongoing relationship with His beloved Son in whom He is well pleased.

And should you choose, please join me in the "worth-ship" (Strong's G4352, worship) that is soon to follow. (My understanding of worth-ship is an all-out, unrestricted, and unlimited declaration from you to God delivered to Him via the vehicle of your best understanding of agape love; simply stated, your most extravagant expression of His worth to you.

It is the prayer of a wimp, but probably not the one you just thought of. This particular meaning is an acrostic that signifies W (work), I (in), M (Messiah's), P (process). And without the enabling power of the Holy Spirit, we will represent the impotent wimp that has never once demonstrated the boldness (Acts 4:13, 29, 31) demonstrated by the newly established church of Acts 2 and beyond. And the worst is that we could sit in the pew for many years and, like the unprofitable servant (Matt. 25:14–30), fail to grow the kingdom by even one soul because we choose to bury the talent that we so freely received. Refuse to let that happen, ok?

As for me, I have decided to make a conscious decision to do my part to fulfill God's desire that none perish (2 Peter 3:9) by doing my very best to fulfill the destiny set before me so I may reasonably approximate Jesus's statement to the Father in His priestly prayer of John 17:4, "I have glorified you on the earth, I have finished the work which you gave me (Mike Rogers) to do."

Will you please consider joining me in verbalizing the following prayer? And I kindly encourage you to substitute your name wherever you feel it to be appropriate. And please keep ever in the forefront of your mind that you were created for dominion: (Gen. 1:26), and by appropriating three priceless gifts(Salvation, the Holy Spirit, and the Holy Bible), you can fulfill the destiny that God determined before the foundation of the cosmos (world). And finally-and oh so absolutely essential-your path will be directed by your very own personal spirit guide, the person of the Holy Spirit (John 14:16–17, 26, 16:13). May we begin ?

> Oh, righteous Father, I have only begun to grasp
> the endless depths of your loving kindness (Ps.
> 136). As I sit here alone, resting in your presence,

I am totally overcome by the realization that there are untold billions of galaxies, each containing billions of stars. And not only do you count the number of those stars, but incredibly you call them by their name (Ps. 147:4). And then I am drawn to recall that you record in your Book of Life the name of every single human who has determined to return himself or herself to you by choosing to receive the most extravagant gift ever offered to mankind (John 3:16–17). And if that were not enough, I recall that you engraved on the palms of your hands the name of every person who accepts the free gift offered in John 3:16 (Isa. 49:16). Further I am compelled to remember that this gift was guaranteed before even one star was brought into existence (Rev. 13:8). Then I revisit the first five days of your Genesis creation and cannot help but notice that you created every single need for this Adam, your finest creature, that you would choose to bring into existence on the sixth day, the one created in your image and after your likeness (Gen. 1:26). Considering these few evidences of your character, how could I possibly fail to agree to pray, "Thy kingdom come, thy will be done, on earth, just as it is in heaven." And knowing full well that you are no respecter of person (Acts 10:34), how could I possibly fail to tell even one of your choice creation that you intentionally place in my path about the indescribably wonderful and most satisfying intimate relationship ever afforded mankind? And I further bask in joyous celebration with the absolute certainty that you will gloriously overshadow every individual who sincerely searches (Phil. 3:10) for the one source of joy that never runs dry. May not even one hour ever pass in which I am not prompted by you through the person of the Holy Spirit to bask in the exuberant joy of being in your presence (Ps. 16:11b). And thank you so very much for your incessant listening and speaking, Abba Father. Oh, how I look forward to our ongoing conversation and subsequent collaboration. In joyous anticipation, I rest expectantly in the midst of your indescribable presence.

With ever increasing love,
Mike Rogers
By choice, a work in the Messiah's process

# About the Author

The author is fully enamored with the lifestyle, compassion, and teaching of the master teacher of all time, has immersed himself in all 66 books of The Great King 28 times, determined to be a disciple of and friend to, Jesus of Nazareth. While he has not attended "preacher's school", his great joy would be to deserve similar recognition accorded to Peter and John in Acts 4:13b, "they took knowledge of them, that they had been with Jesus". Mike is a recipient of the Global University Teaching Certificate for the Christian Service Curriculum, has been a male guide in the pro-life activities of the South Texas Pregnancy Care Center, serves in the local food pantry, led a small group for 7+ years, a part of youth ministry since 1998, consistently taught the word since 2000, and continuously involved in children's ministry since 2002. Missionary trips to Jamaica, Kenya and Mexico hyper-intensified his compassion. He and his wife Cindy are gifted with four delightful daughters, Denise, Diana, Crystal, and Brooke, 6 grandchildren, and 1 great-grandchild. Mike and Cindy currently live in Seguin, Texas, but eagerly anticipate the construction of a Spirit-directed "oasis" in Sutherland Springs, Texas with their 1 dog & 1 cat.

Printed in the United States
By Bookmasters